THREE
DAY
PASS

BEHO,
BREAKTHROUGH,
BATTLES BEYOND.

CAPT. JAMES V. MORGIA

THREE DAY PASS

BEHO, BREAKTHROUGH, BATTLES BEYOND

CAPTAIN JAMES V. MORGIA

•

MASTERY, LLC

Mastery, LLC
21 Tuckahoe Road
Trumbull, CT 06611
masteryllc.co

Third Edition: May 2017
jamesvmorgia.com

The author has endless gratitude for those that played a part in the subsequently mentioned periods of his life. He has, therefore, mentioned them by name in honor of the roles they played for himself and the pivotal moments during World War II. They are also mentioned for historical reference.

Additional information on these individuals may at some point be hyperlinked to electronic versions of this publication to widen their historical reference. Those who are mentioned, or those in their immediate family may have the right to withhold information.

PREFACE

In life, an individual is confronted by challenges that may or may not have been caused by that individual's own actions but must be dealt with pragmatically. Because I believe each individual has the power within to shape the outcome, how that individual deals with the situation, hence, greatly influences the outcome. The individual, in this regard, is at the center of the universe and should accept each challenge with the hope to achieve a favorable outcome. I am both a scholar of science and a believer in God the almighty; maker of heaven and earth. This story is about the experiences in my life and focuses on my ultimate test; the challenge presented to me at a time when I did not expect it or believe I could have been ready for it. My faith in God and country inspired me to persevere in a desperate situation.

Counter to some popular belief, the U.S. Army is an organized, efficient, and effective force intensely loyal to its underlings. I must say I always admired it and in some ways look upon my service in World War II as some of the most exhilarating times in my life.

The U.S. Army is composed of a complex hierarchy structure from the Division at the top of the hierarchy all the way down to the Squad units. Each Division is comprised of three Regiments and each Regiment is comprised of three Battalions. Each Battalion has four Companys of which one was under my command. Each Company consists of four Platoons. And lastly, each Platoon is comprised of three squads. The Regiment is the most important unit in the army. The reason being is that it is essentially a do-it-yourself organization. The Regiment becomes a "task force" when the Division commander's assign Artillery, Engineers, and other support units to be controlled by the Regimental commander. The leader has direct control of all the units to execute a complex mission. Importantly, the command does not need to order outside help which, most of the time, is not ready to mesh with the mission. So, it was the "Task Force Church" (named after Brigadier General John Church) or the RCT (regimental combat team) which operated under Church. These commanders were unlike the high command in that they conducted flexible operations meaning they had power to move men and machinery in a short notice of time. The commanders had an "objective" with many moving parts. Different battles throughout history could be said to be similar, but no two are the same. An analogy is that the objective is to make a touch-down and as the team moves down field, the plays are adjusted accordingly to realize the objective. The commander is more quarterback than symphony conductor. Therefore, warfare is controlled chaos; unpredictable at best with no real order or rhythm. Soldiers had to step into the moment and survive with what was in front of them and use what was available to them thus requiring high degrees of resourcefulness. I guess that is why I had such an affinity for the army as I grew-up in the Depression and was required to be resourceful to survive and prosper.

My E Company story is also published in two other books, In the Footsteps of the Band of Brothers by Mr. Larry Alexander, a columnist for the Intelligencer Journal in Lancaster, Pennsylvania. As well as Gouvy-Beho by Mr. Joseph Neysen; a retired executive with the Michelin tire company.

As with any story there are multiple viewpoints. I will keep my eyewitness accounts as accurate as possible while offering to interject through others' personal accounts where appropriate – supplemented through letters, images, and excerpts. My hope is that the events in this book, that occurred over 70 years ago, give the reader a sense of what war is but in a different time and the struggles that drives one to persevere in times of little hope and despair. Make no mistake, it was a time of wide-spread pessimism in the world and we were at the doorstep of the Axis powers – just meters away from Germany and facing a desperate, focused enemy hell-bent on defending their homeland. It would later be termed "The Battle of the Bulge"; a major turning-point in World War II where the Allies ultimately defeated the Axis powers. With the stroke of grace for those that made it home and with levels of connection that I would feel remiss if left out.

Like most soldiers of World War II, when it came to an end on those decisive days such as VE Day and VJ Day, we went back to our home towns in America as I did to pick-up where we left off. As I had to leave the University of Connecticut for Europe before graduating and upon my return home, I finished my studies to earn a Bachelor of Science degree in Chemistry. After that having sufficient credit to continue my schooling, the army compensated us to continue our education for free. I earned a Master's Degree in Chemistry at New York University in Manhattan in June 1949. I then proceeded to work at my first job, fall in love with my wife, settle in the suburbs, and made a good living as a chemical engineer raising five children.

Every year the 84th Railsplitter Society ran a convention in cities around the U.S. My wife and I would attend these conventions around the country where it was convenient for us to travel to. These conventions were the only place the war was ever discussed. The comraderie never faded with my brother's-in-arms. But as the years went by, the numbers of those brothers began to diminish. Health issues beset by after-war lifestyles took their toll on many of my war buddies as the war never had. Growing up, my children never heard a word from me about any part of the war discussed in this book.

In fact, in 1974, I gave away all my Nazi memorabilia to a local war collector for free. I had items consisting of knives, pistols, flags, etc taken from dead Nazi's. The Army allowed us to take whatever we wanted and bring home in our footlockers. At the time we just thought of them as souvenirs; items taken from our dead foes to symbolize our victory. Not until when I was in retirement and had time on my hands to dwell on the war years did my children ever know details of my time in battle. Also with the aging of The Greatest Generation, historians and lovers of battle tales and logistics were thirsty to hear first-hand accounts from soldiers before their voices were silenced. Oral histories were begun to be recorded. Mine is in the National Archives. Even a WWII memorial was finally built in Washington, DC in 2004 in recognition that our numbers were dwindling at approximately 1,000 old soldiers each day.

I, being a WWII veteran still in good health and sound mind, began to be contacted through the wonders of the internet. A man named Reg Jans contacted me and we began an enduring friendship. He told me how he was making a living giving tours of the very grounds where we fought our historical battles in early 1945 to retake Beho. Reg, in turn, gave my name to others who were making documentaries and writing their own books about WWII. I provided valuable, first-hand accounts to provide authenticity to their books. I discovered that many found my story to be interesting. My story aired April 13, 2013 on the America Heroes Channel episode: "Holding The Line".

Everything that I had learned and endured at the ripe old age of 22 made me prone to have the outcome of my encounter with the Germans to weigh heavily in my favor. It turns out with no commanding office to give me orders or a high-ranking general micro-managing me, as Company Commander, I initiated an attack plan effective and flexible enough to meet any plausible situation and exact a positive outcome for the Allied forces. After receiving the Silver Star for bravery in action, it prompted the Command to replicate my strategy of speed and stealth which was instrumental in bringing the war to a quicker close and, hence, saving both

Allied and German lives. Before I decided on my own to initiate my offense on the Germans at 5 am, all battles started at 9 am after breakfast. I do not know who created this battle strategy but I knew that good men were dying on both sides and a strategy that addressed minimizing exposure time was the best strategy. I must thank my father, Umberto, who never talked much but led by example. He would never let me forget that "the early bird gets the worm". This philosophy no doubt was ingrained in him as he lived on a farm in Italy until coming to the U.S. in 1915 and continued to rise with the chickens each day in Bridgeport, Connecticut.

After Beho, I noticed a shift in the general's thinking; they started to use the element of surprise. The generals became more strategic in their maneuvers. They planned more and if the plan went awry, they did not hesitate to postpone or scrub the mission. I'd like to believe after Beho, I was given safer assignments as rewards for giving them a great tool for at least throwing the enemy off their game- the element of surprise.

Changing things up, never letting the enemy see all your cards, proved effective. They entrusted me with the responsibility of PX duty. I handled all the provisions. They took me off the front lines and out of harm's way.

So why write this book; another war story we have heard before perhaps? It is, of course, about the war but as I wrote it, I began to realize many parallels outside of my war days and how it shapes a person's outlook on life and one's sense of duty. Duty to the Army; your family; your work. I had escaped death a few times as you will read about in this book. Maybe it was fate. Maybe my experiences taught me to be hopeful and that one's greatest work was yet to be achieved and that heroes can exist in each of us and not exclusively on the battlefield. Using my recollections along with historical text, I have compiled for my children, grandchildren, and future great grandchildren a memoir on a life of perseverance, tenacity, and intellect.

May there come a period in man's existence when war stories never have to be written again to be passed down from parent to child.

I wrote this book so others could learn and not be doomed to relive history because they had not learned lessons from the past.

I hope you enjoy my story.

Sincerely,

Capt. James V. Morgia

CHAPTER 1

LT. W. W. THOMPSON'S
THREE DAY PASS TO PARIS

World War II saw many sacrifices for both soldiers in direct combat and civilians caught in collateral damage. Across many cultures and countries, the war became a great unifier of peoples whose mission in life was to support the war effort. In my family, my brother and I were enlisted in the army. My mother worked in the brass shop converted over to make flashlights for soldiers. My father operated a magnetic crane to allow metal to be recycled and converted into war machines. We recycled just about everything. This was the sacrifice for a world faced with an aggression that presented a threat to political and economic stability. Thinking back, no one really understood the implications of what we faced as a country. Coming off a long and stubborn Depression, people were happy just to have a job. Beyond the uncertainty, we pushed forward leading the world through darkness to the glimmer it holds today.

I had always done well in school and knew that I wanted to be an engineer of some type. I was accepted to the University of Connecticut at the Storrs campus. When I joined the ROTC program on campus, the United States was not at war although Europe was engaged in battles with Nazi Germany. The U.S. had a generally isolationist policy and still remembered World War I; we were just trying to stay out of the fray. What abruptly ended this policy, of course, was the bombing of Pearl Harbor by the Japanese in December 1941. That act of war unleashed one of the greatest war machines in the history of the world. Our entire country immediately went into "War" mode the likes of which had to even surprise those who would become our allies. Food was rationed, women gave up their nylons and just painted fake seams onto the back of their legs to give the appearance of nylons, war bonds were sold by actors before movies, women replaced men going off to war in factories and sports teams just to keep everything running at home while young men ran off to war in droves. There was no question as to whether it was the politically correct thing to do but the only thing to do. No men from "The Greatest Generation" ran off to Canada opposing the war. The United States may have been reluctant to get into World War II and for good reason but once we got in, we were in it to win it.

At ROTC, I was whisked-off to officer candidate school at Camp Legeune in Georgia for 4 weeks of basic training. It was here that I met up with the man who would be my commanding officer and friend for life, Lt. William W. "Tommy" Thompson. He was a smooth-talking son of an oil company executive in Waynesboro, Pennsylvania. He and I were raised complete polar-opposites but we formed a fast and enduring friendship and brotherhood that spanned five decades until his death in 2003. I do not think he had ever met anyone like me and vice-versa. I loved him like an older brother I never had.

My story could not have been born if Lt. Thompson, company commander for E Company 334th Infantry Regiment, 84th Division was not ordered to take a three day Paris pass. Lt. Thompson deserved that three-day pass. He earned it by saving his entire platoon from a possible ambush and certain death by the Nazis while traversing the Ardennes forest. There my 72-hour long gauntlet began. Navigating a group of young men across enemy lines and countless unsettling adversities, under the leadership of their new commander, an inexperienced new lieutenant with an ROTC background to rise-up in the ranks overnight.

My first day in command was January 17, 1945. It was E Company's first rear area rest since fighting an offensive action to push the German Troops out of the Ciele, Belgium area (see map). We took many casualties and desperately needed rest and regrouping to fight as a full-strength Company. The town of Barvaux, Belgium (see map) became our momentary sanctuary of much needed rest on January 17, 1945.

We both started with E company, 334 infantry, 84th Infantry Division on November 17, 1944 by attacking the Siegfried line in the Geilenkirken area, near Holland. On the first day of the attack, E Co. lost most of its leaders and Lt. Thompson became the new Company commander and I became the executive officer. We spent the whole month overcoming German troops and destroying pillboxes. The distance covered during this time was about 2 miles. The Germans were very well organized and gave up very little ground. We all spent a lot of time in fox holes which we dug with our collapsible shovel. The weather was generally cold and rainy. Some of us covered the foxhole with a poncho which was waterproof. The German pillboxes were attacked, captured and destroyed. The only relaxation that company E had was spending several days in the basement of a school building in Geilenkirken to get cleaned up. I remembered that we did that several times. On December 17, 1944, in the vicinity of the Roer River, we were mounted on trucks and ended up in Marche, Belgium. To block the German troops advance into Belgium. This later became known as the Battle of the Bulge.

For over two weeks, the E Company troops held the attacking Germans back on a front from Marche to Hotton with other elements of the 84th Division. The next two weeks the 84th Division and other allied troops pushed the Germans back to where they started a month earlier. Someone had a camera and took several pictures of myself and Lt. Thompson and battlefield commission Lt. Clyde Laurent. Attached are those pictures.

It did not take long after Lt. Thompson left for Paris that I was ordered to meet with the newly assigned Battalion Commander, Lt. Col Leonard Umanoff, for the 2nd Battalion of the 334th Infantry. Lt. Col Umanoff replaced former Battalion Commander, Lt. Col. Williams but had very little experience as an infantry leader in theater. This newly assigned battalion commander had little experience on the battlefield with the 84th Infantry Division. He was a replacement directly from the West Point Teaching Staff. He would be used "on and off" to replace former E Company Commanders who were injured in battle.

Now it appears that two leaders needed to combine their military knowledge to make the right moves. But, I must admit, as an Executive Officer for E Company I had never been part of a tactical meeting or even close to commanding an infantry Company. The executive officers usually were the Company commander's "helper" and never issued orders or commands in the deployment of soldiers.

In this world of might and martial action we were starting with a "sub-par" position. We needed all the luck we could get. As if in alliance with the Axis powers, the weather was extremely unforgiving with unrelenting sub-zero temperatures and excess snow which made it very difficult for any offensive group to maneuver. The Nazi forces felt secure and emboldened in the positions they held.

Late in the afternoon of January 21, it was necessary for the battalion Company officers to go on reconnaissance to an area of woods near the Town of Halconreax. This reconnaissance was necessary and is typical so that as troops are brought in, the lay of the land is known and would go towards minimizing casualties. The pine trees were heavily loaded with snow and it was very quiet and cold with a bright sun that didn't make it past the snow-covered obstacles to warm us below. After returning from the reconnaissance mission, everyone in my Company was alerted to prepare for a night in a forested area between Cortil and Halconreaux. Our equipment

329ᵗʰ Regiment, Cortil.

Lt. James Morgia , Barvaux, Be. 1944.

Lt. Thompson, Laurent, Morgia, Barvaux, Belgium, January 16 1944.

and personnel accompanied the unit and prepared a hot meal for everyone on the mission. It was a time of short-lived solace before deployment.

The reason why I indicated that we started the three day venture in a "sub-par" personnel strength was that all of the original platoon leaders for the four E Company platoons were removed from previous engagements with the enemy. Now, only two newly field commissioned officers, Lt. Marvin Jamison and Lt. Clyde Laurent, were made available to manage the two platoons; the 2nd and 3rd. The other two platoons had sergeants as their leaders.

We were leaders for the 84th E Company Platoons - removed from previous engagements with the enemy - now about to be deployed to the snow-capped forest where we only viewed the stately pines as potential instruments for cover under expected enemy fire. Only two newly field commissioned officers, Lt. Marvin Jamison and Lt. Clyde Laurent, were made available to manage the two platoons; the 2nd and 3rd. The other two platoons had sergeants as their leaders.

I must admit that 1st Lt. Thompson commanded E Company on an "off-and-on" basis to replace former E Company commanders who were injured in action. I was an executive officer that took care of the needs of the Company's men; such as, feeding and supplying other necessities required to be battle-ready. At times when it was necessary to contact them in their foxholes during the night, I would commonly encounter a voice from the foxhole asking "What is the password?" I would sometimes forget and respond to the voice "I forgot the password" and the soldier in the foxhole would reply, "It's okay, Lt. Morgia, I recognize your voice!" We knew each other. We always covered each other. We were all in the same situation; too young and too far from our families. There was no way to communicate with mom, dad, or our siblings except through the monthly mail call.

None of us ever spoke of not making it back home alive for fear of demotivating the "machine" that only ran smoothly if all the "parts" worked. We all knew in our minds the odds were greatly against us. We didn't have the home team advantage. We didn't know exactly where we were. We didn't know the enemy's capability except that we were desperately close to their homeland border and were ready for the greatest battle the War had ever known. So, we focused our energies and became each other's surrogate brothers; the band of brothers made up of a mix of American cultures. Me, the son of Italian immigrants who migrated 30 years before. In a strange land with nothing but what we were able to carry with us and our will to survive. At that moment I got a real appreciation for my parents who came to the U.S. during WWI.that moment I got a real appreciation for my parents who came to the U.S. during WWI.

Lt. Laurent, Raymond, Morgia in Barvaux, Belgium, Jan. 16 1944.

CHAPTER 2

PREPARATION AND MOVE
TO BEHO, BELGIUM

O n the morning of January 22, 1945, E Company's 334th
Infantry was positioned in the woods adjacent to the town
of Cortil. The E Company kitchen soldiers and cooks were
also present to serve a hot breakfast for the approximately one hundred
fifty soldiers. Our mission for today was to advance to the town of Beho
in Belgium in a coordinated attack with other forces of the 2nd Battalion,
334th Infantry. We needed to complete this objective for the very simple
reason: to remove the German's from Belgium. Beho was the last town they
occupied in Belgium. We could not wait for Lt. Thompson to return from
Paris. The Germans were on the move back to their homeland because
their mission was in jeopardy and their sole new objective was now to inflict
as many casualties as possible among the Allied troops. The Germans had

taken approximately 60,000 American lives alone in only one month!

I was now leading my Company into some of the most aggressive fighting of the war.

Newly appointed Lt. Col. Umanoff joined my company in the town of Halconreaux and we both led E Company eastward through the snow towards the town of Beho. En route, we were informed that F Company was pinned down by German fire in the area ahead and were unable to maneuver. The Colonel suggested that we "save" F Company and I advised against it. Tactically, my assessment of the situation was that we should not expose ourselves which would put both E and F Company's at an unacceptable level of risk. In hind sight this was the right decision as the German troops occupied the high ground in the Gouvy area and, hence, had a superior advantage. Since E Company was, in fact, very close to German positions on its right flank, intervention would have possibly ended its mission to maneuver elsewhere. Life lesson: Pick your battles. F Company ultimately waited until nightfall to move to their objective; Beho. F Company stayed in their position in the Beho area in reserve status. The Battalion commander made the decision to keep them inactive on the chance they would be needed if the battle of Beho became overwhelming. They were never called up but we joined forces later when we made our move to the Netherlands to get back to the highly fortified Siegfried line.

Lt. Umanoff and I were witnessing as the Germans were firing upon F Company. We quickly discussed our next move. I strongly recommended to Col. Umanoff that we could get to Beho by way of the large area of woods located to our north. He agreed but wanted to go there directly from our current position; a move which I disagreed with because we would make E Company exposed and vulnerable. My instincts dictated that E Company should return to our starting point in the town of Halconreaux and proceed to the woods through a defilade passage. I felt this was a sound strategy by studying the map we were provided by the engineers of the topography of the area. I studied map reading during my time at the UConn ROTC. Lt. Umanoff again agreed with my rationale. Getting to Halconreaux took more time but was the lower-risk alternative. Ultimately, we all got safely to the woods without the Germans spotting us. Although some U.S. artillery fire dropped nearby during our movement, we suffered no casualties

This was the beginning of a series of decisive moves - a game of subtle balance wherein the smallest differences in strategy could have devastating consequences leaving no room for error. A mathematical conundrum where game theory met practical application.

Once in the woods, around 1400 hours (2 pm), it was agreed that we would follow the railroad tracks through the wood's eastern edge which was close to Beho, our prime objective. Of course, how to find the snow-covered railroad leading to Beho was our overarching concern. We deployed two scout parties comprised of three soldiers each that took two separate paths heading north. The scout report later returned that indeed the railroad tracks were, in fact, as shown on the Army-issued map. Lt. Col. Umanoff ordered me to lead E Company on the tracks to our objective.

The original Regimental plan was that E Company would participate in attacking Beho with other units of the 334th Regiment at 1700 hours (5 pm). From our position in the woods, we could hear the bombardment of the town by our own artillery which was successful in driving-out the German troops from Beho. These German troops were not the same that occupied Gouvy. Due to the snow and ice conditions our progress was slow and we emerged at approximately 2100-2200 hours from the woods onto the N-69, a main road. We did not know at the time but the railroad tracks and roads were sprinkled with anti-personnel mines which were impossible to detect. I discovered later from a letter by Lt. Charles D. Raymond, Battalion G-4 Supply Officer that the deep freeze helped E Company get through without detonating mines as the ground was frozen. The cold obviously did have an advantage. It saved our lives.

Since E Company arrived in Beho late, there were no available spots in or near town to settle in for the night. The men of E Company had only blankets and white camouflage outer cover sheets to spend the night in the snow covered field outside Beho. Noone really slept much as the fear was if you slept, you may not wakeup

succumbing to the cold. An interesting letter was sent to me many years after the War from Lt. Raymond in which he shared that the horse and buggy he had borrowed which carried all the blankets were destroyed by mines on the N-69 road near Beho. He used such primitive local equipment to deliver wool blankets to the G.I.'s on the front line. The horse and buggy were heavy enough to detonate the mines.

In general, mechanized vehicles were not effective during the American Offensive in this theater. The roads were icy and slick, the temperatures too low, and the forests too thick. This battle was a true infantry-led effort; men carrying backpacks and hiking to their objectives. It was a problem for the infantrymen and it took impromptu innovation to hold our positions.

Frost bite was a major concern with exposed skin freezing in 30 seconds. Many soldiers discarded their overcoats instead opting for many layers of clothing. Generally, extra undershirts and combat jackets were used. Dry sock availability kept the dreaded trench feet problems at manageable levels. Of course, we all must think of Lt. Raymond's dedicated personal attention to detail with his S-4 Battalion team in keeping the men supplied with wool blankets and variable food rations no matter what the harsh environment that was encountered. It was a battle on its own and aided in the success and longevity of infantrymen throughout the War.

CHAPTER 3

THE BATTLE OF BEHO

Day 3 started at 0200 hours because I was ordered to attend a meeting with the 2nd Battalion Commander Lt. Col. Umanoff. I had very little sleep so to speak of since Thompson's three day pass started. The objective given to me was to take the high ground around Beho was ordered to a battalion headquarters meeting with Lt. Col Umanoff for the objective assignment. E. Company was to take the high ground overlooking the town of Beho. This area was about 1,000 yards due east of Beho. F Company was to remain in reserve status. G Company, under Capt. Hyatt, was to take a wooded area just south of the E Company objective. F Company was to remain in reserve status and remained in town. I struggled to stay awake during the meeting and the Lt. Col made sure that I understood the assignment.

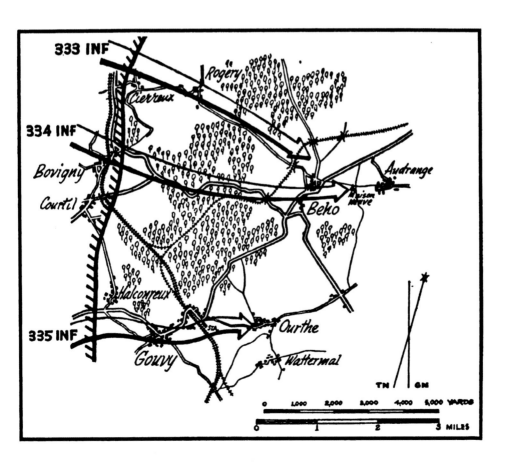

I realized that I must assemble the E Company men as quickly as possible. I directed the platoon leaders, 2nd Lt. Claude Laurent, Jr., who was newly field commissioned 3rd platoon and 2nd Lt. Marvin Jamison who was also newly field commissioned 2nd platoon and two unnamed platoon leaders (non-commissioned) for 1st and 4th platoon to a short meeting.

I ordered the platoon leaders to prepare their men to cross the Line of Departure (L.D.) near the four corners (the intersection N68 and N827) at 0600 hours, to start moving to high ground overlooking the town of Beho. Since, nothing was known of the area we would dig-in and hold that position. The only map available was created by 654th US Army Engineers, US Army, 1944. At the Initial Point (I.P.), I met an officer from the division artillery who was waiting for F Company commander to which he was assigned and would not need an artillery Field Observer (F.O.) that day. I told him it was impossible for him to join F Company and I coaxed him to join E Company since we would need an F.O. if we encountered German Troops. He could have disobeyed my plea (I could not order him since he did not belong to E Company). My argument compelled him to reluctantly join our column. Since all the orders were verbal, he was in fact supposed to be with E Company but was incorrectly assigned to F Company. He proved to be invaluable as his training was key in the coming battle.

In general, we had very limited information about mounting an offensive and we were not told about the enemy situation or anything. We were totally in the dark about what to expect. And, once we got there; what to do. Unbeknownst to me at the time, "luck" was going to play a very important role in our success at the end of the day.

I, as a lieutenant, acting as both company commander and executive officers and, led approximately 150 men of E Company forward at about 0600 hours (6 a.m.). As a general rule of engagement, battles were begun at 0900 hours (9 a.m.). Drawing on my knowledge of history, I rationalized that a tactic used by General

George Washington was the right plan…engage the enemy earlier than they would expect and catching them asleep and off-guard. In retrospect, the early morning wake-up call really increased our chances for success. The cover of darkness also helped to keep our casualties down; you cannot shoot what you cannot see. Unlike today where night vision equipment is common. The single-file column was led upward through over waist high snow covered terrain, there was no indication of pathways or roads on the terrain we were traversing. It was tough going and the trek took several hours.

It was pitch dark that night with no moon to light our way. Of course, no flashlights could be used as this would potentially give away our position. It was also extremely cold with temperatures of minus 20 Fahrenheit. I had no compass and my only guide was the terrain itself. Since the objective was the high ground, I knew I must keep walking uphill. Everyone actually followed in my path created in the deep snow. The column of troops was started approximately 50 yards behind me. This also was unusual for a Company commander to lead his men on a mission. Scouts were typically used to go and report back to them informing of the situation and certainly no drones at that time or GPS. I, on the other hand, was the Commander, leader, and scout all-in-one. This was do-it-yourself but in battle conditions. The situation required rapid movement to the objective because we could not afford to be discovered on our way which would have trapped us helpless should we come under enemy fire. There was really no time or none of my superiors present to discuss this operation any further. We got only basic orders and it was on me to formulate the execution plan…we were on our own.

The entire countryside was absolutely free of sounds. Nothing was moving. I felt an uneasy calm in this silence; thinking back, there was no palpable feeling of fear. It is difficult to explain but in the moment, doubt can easily lead to death of you and your men. Moving further upward, I caught sight of a building; a stone farmhouse that seemed uninhabited. As I approached it, I passed close by a German sentry without knowing it except "feeling" a movement on my right side. After passing the sentry, the silence was broken by him challenging me with a command, "Halten Sie!". I immediately ran diagonally and away from him to present to him a much more difficult "target" to hit. He fired his rifle at me and missed. I tried to fire back with my carbine but it jammed. After this exchange, the sentry disappeared into the darkness leaving his post. At that moment I felt the adrenaline and was sure the sentry would call for back-up and that we would soon be under assault. I had to assume that he would not think I was alone. I thought to myself "Halt Hell" and I yelled to my troops, about 50 yards away and stretched for 200 yards, "Let's Go!!. This war cry would later be the title of the article in the Bridgeport Post that reported the story back home on March 02, 1945. The sentry would have been ordered to watch the road looking west to the town of Beho. We, however, approached from a different direction. Until that moment of discovery by the sentry, we arrived the German party early and unnoticed; not to mention uninvited.

"Halt Hell; Let's Go, War Cry Bridgeporter Routs the Enemy"

accounting the entire battle and reported I was awarded the Silver Star for bravery. (See reference news account at end of the chapter).

Thinking back to that moment when I was challenged by the sentry, I was not sure if the sentry thought there was only me in the area or if any other American soldiers were there with me regardless if I was alone, he would have to assume I could call back for reinforcements or call in his position. I would never know if having my troops (E Company) far enough behind me may have caused the sentry to believe I was alone providing more time for my troops to complete their trek and join me but the right thing to do was to assume he thought I was not alone and to prepare for retaliation. At that point, it made no difference the commotion my men made to rapidly advance and group to take the next order. This was now a full raid on the enemy. After the snow-suit covered men quickly moved to join me, I assigned each platoon a separate farm building to occupy and hold. This was our stated objective! The Germans were completely surprised waking them from there night's sleep. Discovered, they were fleeing the farm houses for their Mark IV Panzer Tiger tanks and vehicles nearby.

The Easy Company, 334th objective was instantly determined when the German sentry challenged me with his command. He was standing quietly behind a low wall beside a building which I really did not notice because it was so dark. I may have been walking across a paved road but with all the snow the landscape was uniformly covered and made it impossible to determine what map topography was and where. In hindsight, if the guard had not challenged me, I could have missed stopping at this point. Essentially, I knew we were in the correct location due to this sentry. We just did not know exactly what the strength and number of German's we engaged.

The two lead platoons, 2nd and 3rd, led by newly battle field commissioned, 2nd Lt. Marvin Jamison and 2nd Lt. Clyde Laurent were directed to occupy two separate farm buildings nearby. The 4th weapons platoon was instructed to setup their mortars and machine guns near the rear of the farmhouse facing east. I next took the last (1st platoon) with me and rushed head long towards the farmhouse. I rushed headlong into the direction of the house and tossed a hand grenade through the window into the entrance room. There were no Germans here but were sleeping in the barns. I rushed to the second floor to find a window to view the outside in an easterly direction. I had a narrow view and could hear small arms fire outside and the loud rumbling of Mark IV shells impacting the all-stone farm structures that we occupied. The tables were turned; we became the targets.

Each platoon was assigned to enter and occupy each of three barn buildings. The 2nd platoon under 2nd Lt. Marvin Jamison took a barn and 3rd platoon under 2nd Lt. Clyde Laurent, Jr. took the next barn.

The second platoon burst into the barn and ran into more than 20 enemy tankers-soldiers. Tankers were not infantry. They were crew members of the Mark IV's and were not ready to engage hand-to-hand in close quarters. They needed to be in their machines to fight. In the dark they were yelling, a few shots rang out, and some hand-to-hand grappling as the Americans came in one door and the Germans tried to flee out the other.

Once within the farmhouse, and from an observation position on the 2nd floor which I made my makeshift command post (C.P.), I spotted the three German Mark IV Panzer tanks. These massive tanks squatted just 75 yards to the northeast of the farmhouse. Next, they began blasting the buildings with their 88 mm high-velocity shells. The "88's" were unmatched in

Maison Neuve Farm Buildings overlooking Beho.

their destructive power. However, the thick walls of stone absorbed the blasts.

It was becoming daylight now, about 0730 hours. As the shelling continued, it became more apparent that our small arms fire would have no effect on "taking-out" these machines. After destroying; their immediate enemy (us), their next move was to set their sights on Beho; the original objective we had disturbed. My forward observer from artillery Battalion, who was by my side, waited for my direction. We discussed the situation in real time and quickly agreed the artillery was needed as soon as possible. I ordered the forward observer officer to order artillery to disperse the tanks. The F.O. used his personal radio to communicate with the artillery positions which were several thousand yards from our position. Within minutes from calling in our position coordinates, the shells began to rain down closer than 100 yards from us.

Observing the artillery damage was difficult because the farm house had no windows on the North and South side. We could only hear the shells hitting their targets and the surrounding area. Now, around 0800 hours, there was a lull in activity. This was short-lived as at 0900 hours, I spotted trucks in the distance. Men in white snowsuits quickly dismounted their vehicles in a flowing fashion and were approaching us from the East. Since E Company men wore white snow suites, I thought that they were American reinforcements. Raising my field glasses, I focused on the first man, and he was carrying a "burp" gun; the Schmeisser machine pistol. These were German troops on the attack.

We were quickly outnumbered and pinned-down. More German infantry began appearing. Within minutes, my men were taking fire from the north, south, and east directions. Sgt. Issy Lockley recalled that his friend of his second platoon, Sgt. William H. Lumpkin, who was firing his gun from the second floor window in the barn, had a shell blast sweep his helmet from his head. Had his chinstrap been fastened, Lumpkin would most likely have been decapitated. Another, Staff Sergeant William E. Wright, crawled forward within the barn and lay just 30 feet from a machine gun position. Armed with a rifle grenade, he fired it so that the missile burst over the enemies head in a tree-burst fashion, taking-out the gun and crew.

Sgt. Ivan Beams sent me a letter from his winter vacation home in Destin, Florida which gave me a vivid personal description of the action at Maison de Neuve. I cannot write the details like his own story which is presented here:

Dear Jim,

As you requested I am returning your article about the action at Beho. It is very good and a great credit to your leadership that day.

My memory of Beho is "sketchy" at best although I sure remember it was one of the hardest days of combat that E Company faced in the Battle of the Bulge. My platoon must have been toward the rear of the column moving up toward the monastery because I could hear the machine gun a rifle fire before we got all the way there. Just before we came to the big stone barn, there was one of our non-coms crouched behind a stone wall. He was sending our men across a farm lane that was sporadically sprayed with German machine gun fire. He held the column up and sent us across the lane one by one, between bursts of fire. Somehow we all made it into the area behind the barn where there were a few German foxholes. As many of us as could got in the holes while others just had to take whatever cover they could find. In-coming fire was terrific and we were really pinned down. I'm not sure if it was tank or mortar fire, but it was mostly bursting in the trees over our heads and then raining down on the ground all around us. The foxholes seemed pretty exposed to that kind of fire. I'm afraid most of my squad or platoon, (whichever it was), did not have much idea of the big picture, nor even where the fire was coming from.

After we had been there a while one of the non-coms from another platoon crawled out to the hole where I was and said one of the officers wanted someone to go back the way we had come to help some relief from Company F, (I think), to find us and hurry them alng. I went back, moving as fast through the snow as I could. Only a short way from the monastery, a German Panzer tack came out of the woods to my left, across a small ravine and perhaps a hundred yards or so away. I tried to get behind a clump of evergreen trees so the tankers wouldn't see me. But when the tank slowed its pace and the turret began to turn in my direction I didn't wait to see if the had seen me, I took off as fast as I could through the tracks we had made coming up to the monastery.

The tank never did fire and I very soon came upon the relief column coming my way and I was very glad to lead them up to our position. When I got back to the foxhole that I had been in, I found out another soldier had taken my position when I left and he had either been badly wounded or killed, I am not sure which now. Well, that's about what I rember about Beho.

See you soon,

Ivan

Ivan Beams

A letter from Sgt. Ivan Beams. His personal account of Maison Neuve.

The GI's fought in a feverish fashion, slamming fresh ammo clips into the smoking, hungry breeches of their M-1 rifles as fast as they could. The barn was riddled by small arms fire while 88 mm shells from the Panzers pulverized the stone facade of the building.

As the Germans passed closer, we faced the very real danger of being swamped by the 20th Panzer grenadiers. We were in a desperate situation. We could not fight off the in-coming German soldiers. I knew that it was necessary to call for additional artillery down close to our own position and turned to the artillery spotter only to see him emptying a clip from his gun into his own radio. The F.O. said to me "I tell you, this situation looks hopeless. We're in trouble and I can't let the enemy get my radio."

Luckily, I had my own Company radio man and had the radio operator contact Battalion, 2nd, headquarters to order artillery support to fire upon my coordinates utilizing my map. Within a few minutes, the very first artillery 105 mm shell hit the lead truck target with amazing accuracy destroying it and scattering the enemy soldiers. Given that the artillery gun positions were some 3,000 yards away and I was in extreme close proximity from where the first shell landed, the margin for error was extremely small. It was another calculated risk I had to take. If we were all killed by friendly artillery fire it was worth it as the lives of several thousand in the town below would be spared. It was that easy. I had many emotions in my head; I felt both empowered and extremely lucky at that moment but also sick in that I and my men could have been easily killed by friendly fire. It was a risk I had to take. From that day on, I never doubted my map-reading skills!

I also had concurrently ordered my runner, PFC Robert E. Epley, of Gettysburg, PA to run back to the town of Beho and tell them that we need reinforcements to push the Germans back. I needed all the help I could get to keep the Germans from taking the Maison de Neuve area which would bring have put us in harm's way, the approximately 5,000 84th Division troops sheltering within Beho's buildings not to mention the town's residents.

Between the artillery fire and stubborn resistance of Easy Company defending the stone farm buildings, the German attack sputtered out. The Battle of Maison de Neuve was over by 0100 hours, but not without loss.

Two officers Lt. Jamison, 2nd platoon leader and Lt. Clyde Laurent, Jr. 3rd Platoon leader were dead and two enlisted men mortally wounded. PFC Hubert W. Spivey of North Carolina and PFC William F. Lamb of New

York brave heroes to which this book is dedicated to.

At this point of the multiple activities at Maison de Neuve, I never really understood until years later, when my daughter found an article on-line, the reason for the attack by the 20th S.S. Panzer grenadiers. Four German companies and several Mark IV Panzer tanks were involved according to the aforementioned Bridgeport Post article.

It now becomes obvious that the Mark IV tanks positioned behind the Maison de Neuves farm building, although retreating back to the nearby German border also intended to bombard the town of Beho and "crush" units of the 333rd and 334th regiments located in town. Perhaps, this was a standard operating procedure or a planned operation. The reason is simply that in a situation where the enemy forces are retreating on a broad front, a counter attack tactically is a waste of resources. However, since the Mark IV tanks failed to upset the town of Beho, the German high commander skillfully counterattacked the E Company-held Maison de Neuve to attain a position in order to "upset" the battle-wise regiments, 333rd and 334th Infantry Regiments sleeping in town.

There is no doubt in my mind that the German high command knew what the 84th Division line-up would be for the next battle of Germany in the months ahead. I know now that the two 84th Division Generals, General Alexander Bolling and General John Church were grateful for my repelling not one but two major interruptions on the town of Beho. I bring this thought up because an observer of history will think of the battle to save Beho as not one but two major events.

The first event was over when the F.O. attached to E Company shot up his radio and second event began when I picked up my radio. The first event was the dispersion and destruction of the Panzer tanks and the second event was the subsequent attack by the German 30th Panzer grenadiers.

Now I really must point out the importance of the Maison de Neuve interruption. There is no doubt in my mind that the German Mark IV tanks were positioned at the Maison de Neuve Farm area primarily to destroy the town of Beho on the morning of January 23, 1945. The town is approximately 1,000 yards away with no view obstructions in between.

The course of the war was changed by protecting the town of Beho. It should be noted that this author, while doing some background searches for the other authors, Joseph Neysen and Larry Alexander, made a special telephone call to one of his 84th Division Buddies, Pvt. William Fazioli of

Sarasota Springs, NY. He was with I Company, 334th Infantry in the town of Beho during the night of January 22-23, 1945. He remembers that he spent "most of the night" looking for a place to sleep. He found that all the buildings were "wall to wall" occupied with sleeping soldiers.

Pvt. William Fazioli, ended up sleeping on a washing machine. So, when I had stated that I may have saved 5,000 American lives that night by arriving at the Maison de Neuve minutes before the German tankers became alert and active, is an accurate estimation. The facts show that the 84th Division's two regiments 333rd and 334th secured Beho that night of January 22-23, 1945 and saved the troops that took shelter in the homes with the town's estimated 5,000 civilians. These troops were previously identified to support the Task Force Church operation to destroy the Siegfried Line. Losing these highly-trained troops would have compromised the attack and prolong the war.

Using the 84th Division organization information, there is approximately 3,000 men per regiment. Theoretically, 6,000 men sleeping in town. The reason why I discussed the 333rd and 334th Infantry regiments in great detail is simple that these regiments were the great key part of General Bolling's and General Church's forces in the war's greatest breakthrough in the European theater. These leaders really knew the workings of the Siegfried Line. It was undoubtedly the most fortified area known on the planet. It was the last line of defense for the German homeland. It had become infamous to all the Allied soldiers and synonymous with certain death. General Bolling created Task Force Church on February 26, 1945, which consisted of following units:

771st tank battalion (Co A, 334th Infantry, riding on lead tanks) 1st Battalion, 334th Int. (less Company A) motorized

Cannon Co – 334th Infantry 84 Reconnaissance Troop

Company B, 309 Engineers C Battalion 326 Field Artillery (FA) Battalion

Battery D, 557th AAA Anti-Aircraft (AW) (AW) Battalion 326 FA Battalion

Battery D, 557th Anti-AircraftAAA (AW) Battalion 3rd Battalion, 334th Infantry Motorized

Company D Group, 334th Infantry.

Company A, 637 Tank Destroyer Battalion Reinforced Special Units, 334th Infantry

Company B, 309 Medical Battalion 2nd Battalion, 334th Infantry

This was the assembly destined to enter Germany and end the war in Europe. The most compelling thought for this whole campaign had to do with the counter attack ordered by the German high command to the Commander of the 20th Panzer Grenadiers. Undoubtedly, the commander of the 20th Panzer was familiar with the 84th Division's powerful machine and that it would return to the Linnich Roer River area to penetrate his homeland (Germany) rather than "retreat" from the Maison de Neuve complex after silencing of the Mark IV Tanks, whose mission was to "disrupt" the 333rd and 334th Infantry Regiments while they occupied the town of Beho.

Getting back to battle, F Company reinforcements arrived and I took the time to go into the cellar of the farmhouse. I found the Nolle Family, huddled for protection. Pierre, his wife Suzanne, and seven children ranging in ages from 10 years to 16 months old George and his twin sister, Marion Theresa who were all in good condition. We did not speak each other's languages but words were not needed as their gratitude was apparent to see an American soldier to liberate them.

After this meeting, I settled into a deep sleep because I had gone without rest for several days. I still do not remember how I got to the next area of town.

For my actions at Maison-Neuve, I was awarded the Silver Star Medal and got my three day pass to Paris which coincided with the historic and rapid breakthrough from the Roer River to the Rhine River. PFC Robert E. Epley earned a Bronze Medal for his actions.

After the war, Lt. Thompson, PFC Epley, myself, and our wives stayed as close friends throughout the years seeing each other at the yearly reunions held across the U.S.

'Halt, Hell; Let's Go' War Cry, Bridgeporter Routs the Enemy

WITH THE 84TH INFANTRY DIVISION IN BELGIUM—Picked to lead his company in the absence of the commanding officer, a 22-year-old lieutenant discovered that "the old man" does more than pick out command posts. Sometimes he slugs it out with German companies and three tanks.

When his company of the 334th jumped off at 6:30 one dark misty morning, Lieut. James V. Morgia, 903 Pembroke street, Bridgeport, Conn., led his platoons through waist high snow drifts against high ground east of the town of Beho.

Just short of the objective was a cluster of farm buildings, a hurdle he had to jump before he could dig in on the hill.

A few yards before the first building he saw a form in the half light of dawn.

Then: "Halte" as the figure sprang to life.

"Halt, hell," mumbled the lieutenant. "Let's go!" he yelled firing as he ran.

The sentry fired once and disappeared, but it was too late to organize a defense. The snow-covered men of E. Company charged the first two buildings, took them and scrambled for the hill beyond as machine-guns opened up every-where.

Lieut. Morgia ordered his platoons to withdraw inside the buildings while he and the forward observer climbed the stairs to a second story window.

A tank opened fire with machine guns and an "88" at point blank range, but they couldn't see it from the barn.

Coming over the ridge 200 yards away, the observer saw two more tanks and called for artillery. The first round fell short, but the second blew up the lead tank and stopped the second.

"I saw troops marching in columns on the road ahead," said the lieutenant, "at first they looked like Americans in snow capes. Through my field glasses I saw the first man carrying a burp gun. Before I could give order to fire, it seemed as though every man in the company laid fire on that column. We saw the first few men fold and the others broke for cover. I called for artillery that caught them dispersing.

"Meanwhile, the tank we couldn't see had maneuvered into a position to shell the buildings we were in. It opened fire about 50 yards away on the brick wall. We had moved to a room in the middle of the barn and we just huddled on the floor waiting for those damn shells to break through the room.

"Our artillery came in time it fell so close we the barn shake, but it so

"The tank quit and withdrew. They had co the observer emptied a radio figuring we were

Lieut. Morgia and his informed they had foug German companies at a killed and eight wound

BIBLE CLASS TO RED MEN'S S

Everyman's Bible cla serve "Redmen's Sund regular session, Sunday m. in the Y.M.C.A.

The Associated Past S sociation, Red Men of and the Degree of F have been invited to meeting, District 2 inch as follows: Ackenash, 86 ford; Okenuck 49 of Stra wompon 40 and Konck 30 of Bridgeport; Unqu Fairfield and Compo 63 port.

George W. Carey will Scripture and the invoc be by George M. Barnes will introduce the guest Potanovie, will play "R March."

The highest point is Mount Bataan, which ri 4,660 feet.

Lt. Morgia's first-hand account via local news article, March, 1945.

Thr 84th Railsplitter Reunion in Harrisburg, PA, 1975.

CHAPTER 4
THE CRITIQUE

The army had a very good way to train leaders thoroughly by having them "learn by mistakes". After a tactical exercise or engagement, a critique meeting allows the attendees to voice their opinions. In this forum, everyone has an opportunity to voice his constructive criticism of the operation.

There is always room for criticism in that since combat involves many risks and unknowns, the law of probability can heavily influence the outcome. For instance, the field officer's decision to destroy his radio, SCR-#300. In hindsight was not a good one. His emotions controlled his decision-making. Yes, he was following

S.O.P. (Standard Operating Procedure) but was early in executing it. It is known that a good officer follows orders from his commander. This officer's estimate of the situation considered that the 20th SS Grenadier counter attack on the Maison de Neuve was a surprise and E Company soldiers were in serious danger of being neutralized.

I was next to the field observer in our command post (CP) when this happened. The command post was located on the second floor of the farmhouse. The farmhouse was slightly behind the barns.

However, the lucky part of this choice to establish a CP here was that it had a great view of the road leading from the occupied town of Aldringen due east (see map) of our position. This road led to the town of Beho due West. No one expected a counter attack by the German troops, and as I stated before I saw the leading trooper with a burp gun through my field glasses.

Summoning my E Company radioman, P.F.C. George Karas, Waterbury, CT, to contact the 2nd Battalion headquarters and order deployment of artillery to fire on my coordinates was the disruptor of this counter attack. I will never forget the image of the first shell landing on the lead German truck's radiator cap. This was the initiating event that disrupted the counter attack, that ultimately saved E Company, and spared the town of Beho, Gouvy, Belgium. This was indeed a lucky move. The precision and timing could not have been better. The Germans were demotivated and demoralized and had to think seriously where they were treading. I imagine they felt superior as they occupied the high ground but quickly learned otherwise. The overwhelming force the artillery laid on our position was truly devastating. Separate artillery batteries at different locations laid fire on the same target at the same time; truly a devastating display of power I had never witnessed prior. At that moment I felt a deep sense of accomplishment and satisfaction; not to mention…luck. Additional reading on these first-hand accounts can be read in my chapter "Proud to Be a Railsplitter" in Mike Chirco's book "Echoes From a Foxhole", Old Ridge Bookbindery, 1995.

> *Author note: As a lieutenant, the tactic I strategized of beginning an offensive in the pre-dawn hours was previously unpracticed but was noted by and used subsequently by other commanders until the end of the war. The battle to save Beho was selected to be written in detail within the 334th regimental history book "Fortune Favors the Brave" by Perry Wolfe.*

This key initiative could have had a very different outcome if the timing and quick situational awareness had not been present. Yes, I had officer's training and yes I was college educated but I owe my qualities to life experiences since childhood growing up in Bridgeport, CT during the Depression. Many of us had to adopt a Do-It-Yourself attitude about everyday things people typically take for granted. Improvising and work was your life. Leisure was only a concept and if there was time for it, it was of very basic form. No vacations, but stay-cations. Before coming to Belgium I only knew Bridgeport, CT, Fort Benning in Georgia for basic training, and Storrs, CT where I attended UConn in the school of Chemistry and the ROTC.

CHAPTER 5
THE CONNECTION

After the battle to save my Company, I fell asleep on the floor of the farmhouse. The next thing I remembered was being in the town of Houffalize, about 5 miles southwest of Beho, waiting there for several days to assemble troops to return north to Eygelshoven, Holland.

The 334th regimental convoy used red ball express 2 ½ ton trucks to move the men on a secret trip without headlights at night. The Company E convoy of trucks met the mainline of the regimental truck convoy without the last truck of E company group. I was in that last truck with kitchen personnel in back and alongside the driver in a kitchen cook, TEC 5 Sgt. William J. Cesa, Cleveland, Ohio, who was ill. The reason why the last E company truck became missing was due to the hairpin turns of roads in the Houffalize town area where we stayed. The trailer filled with kitchen equipment could not negotiate the sharp turns. It took time with my assistance to work up the ravine in an alternate course. My truck must have been about one hour late for our rendezvous with the main convoy. It was very dark but we drove north.

On this dark night, my truck with the kitchen personnel and a trailer full of kitchen equipment was traveling due north on unmarked roads and without travel lights. It was very quiet and monotonous except when I was whistling to keep the driver alert and when I was humoring my sick kitchen cook. Now and then we would hear a truck-like sound – a buzz bomb guided missile streaking overhead to intended targets in the West.

At the light, we found ourselves stopped by a convoy of trucks across our front. It was not apparent who this convoy was. I stepped out to get information about our location and destination. I saw a tall figure in front with his back towards me and asked, "Sir, what unit is this?" The soldier turned around. It was my company commander, Lt. William W. Thompson. "For cry sake, Lt. Morgia, stop fooling around. I am tired!", he exclaimed. "I was lost all night", I said in response.

We all made it safely to Eygelshoven, Holland.

The Eygelshoven, Holland Area was used as an assembly position for the 84th division troops. The move was made in secrecy – so all shoulder patches and unit insignia were removed. The townspeople billeted the men in neat houses. All the Dutch civilians were very friendly. Some of the G.I.'s had taken extra food from the kitchen's chow line to feed families with whom they were billeted. I had a picture taken of myself outside one of these homes.

Morgia outside of a Netherlands house, Feb. 1945.

Importantly enough, we later found that the Germans knew we were there and the German broadcasting element from radio Arnheim "welcomed" the 84th Infantry Division back to the ninth Army front the day after our arrival. I have a good idea that the German High Command (GHC) concluded this scenario when the Battle of the Bulge was coming to a close. The huge counterattack that we witnessed at the Maison de Neuve farm complex was an attempt by the GHC, seeing the end insight, to annihilate the 333rd and 334th Regiments sheltered within the homes of Beho below. The timing of the German counterattack was very early in the day of January 23, 1945, after the three Mark IV tanks "parked" at the Maison de Neuve were routed by E company earlier. The 20th SS Panzer Grenadier 200 troops and other Mark IV tanks reinforcements were stopped with our artillery curtain. The 84th troops suffered minimal casualties.

One may be able to comprehend a physical connection to the 84th Infantry Division and its position on the Siegfried front and its move to the Belgian bulge and back again – facing the German defenses at the Geilenkirken area. However, it is a larger stretch to imagine a more covalent connection. One that is invisible, unspoken, but on the same wavelength. What happened at Beho became an echo for everyone's ego for the role in which we played. That is the reason for me to write this account. From my calculations and understanding, the movement of troops, the war in Europe was shortened by at least 30 days. The 84th Infantry Division made a significant difference that only the correct timing and character could make. The circumstances came together in a way that could not have been planned by any high-ranking officer nor by anyone without foresight of what was to likely happen. We all played our part and I take great satisfaction and humbled knowing that I was instrumental in "sharpening" the Railsplitters' axe. I took this as a life lesson with me after the war into my personal and professional life convinced that the average person can and will make a significant positive difference in the lives of many if the objective is clear and pure.

I still remember the calamity that my Company faced on that very first day of combat in the Siegfried Line, on November 17, 1944 near the town of Geilenkircken. Most of the E Company commissioned officers and non-commissioned officers were killed in action (KIA) or injured. Our Company commander, Capt. James D. Ledbetter, Georgia, was injured in the arm. The assistant commander, 1st Lt. James D. Welsh, Ohio, was runover by friendly tank and 2nd Lt. John. L. Wilson, Waco, Texas and T/ Sgt Lawrence J. Salvato were injured. In addition, the two KIA, that I know of are T/Sgt Vincent Clementi, New Brunswick, New Jersey and Sgt. Loren Hall, Niagra Falls, New York.

I missed being killed-in-action (KIA) by an eyelash. I can still remember every detail after 72+ years. Being a weapons platoon leader, I walked in friendly tank tracks, in an open field looking for targets for my light machine guns and mortars. Half way to my destination, two projectiles whizzed over my head and exploded beyond me. I crouched in the tank track and witnessed two more impacts before me. I knew that I was being "bracketed" by some large caliber fire. Since, the trajectory was low, I thought that it was an "88". These were high velocity shells. The same munitions are used to knock-out tanks or high flying aircraft. I was never personally under such fire before, but I did read about it in army literature.

My immediate action was to move from the "ranged-spot" and seek deeper protection in an "off-range" area. I ran and found an Air Force bomb crater and jumped into the shallow recess. Shortly, thereafter, two more "88"'s hit near the edge of the crater. I remained still for about five minutes. I stuck my head up to see where the firing was coming from and got two more shells in the same spot. The edge of the crater helped to deflect the exploding shell blast upward and avoid hitting me with shrapnel. At this moment I just laid flat with my face up, eyes closed, and played dead. I lay motionless, without moving a single eyelash for twenty minutes or so. My only thought was that some artillery observer ahead of my position was checking the results of his fire mission and if I moved, he would try again to finish his "target". I only knew that I must not look where the firing came from.

After several minutes laying there "lifeless", I looked up to see one of my platoon personnel standing next to me and asked, "Lt. Morgia, what shall I do with this German soldier?" I replied, "Have him walk back to our rear area and someone will take care of him." Later, I found out that the prisoner, was a German field observer, behind our lines calling for artillery to inflict losses for E Company and it was easy to spot the leaders with white band strips on the rear of their helmets. That observer thought that I was dead and was watching me for some time and thought he got me.

The result of the first day of action in the Siegfried Line saw Lt. Thompson promoted to the position of Company commander and myself to assistant company commander or executive officer. We never expected this type of promotion, after our first day of live combat. We were together again as a team. We were now working together, side-by-side. This is a fantastic pairing since we were first brought together about 6 months earlier at Camp Claibourne, Louisiana and lived in a doubles hutment. We were from the opposite ends of the social ladder. His parents were in business and were high on the social ladder in the town area of Waynesboro, Pennsylvania. My parents emigrated from the Rome and Naples areas of Italy and met and married in Bridgeport, Connecticut. Nine months later, I was born as the first son. The armed services was a true a melting pot for all walks of life! Note that Lt. Thompson was an excellent leader and executive type and I was an excellent provider to support the troops.

As I mentioned earlier, after the war, we visited each other and attended many of the Railsplitter Society's yearly conventions. Many other E Company soldiers attended these conventions as well. These were the only times that we talked about our past army experiences. It was very difficult to talk about our war experiences with "civilians" and in some ways was therapeutic for all. As the years passed, the reunions diminished in attendees. The last one I attended was in Saratoga, New York in 1993.

The Lt. Thompson and Lt. Morgia combination made it through all of E Company engagements. Our Company had seen many replacements in our many front engagements. The first engagement period was in the Siegfried Line from November 17, 1944. We were part of the 334th regiment of the 84th Infantry Division's three regiments. During that first period we advanced only one to two miles in the 30 days. The second engagement period was in the Battle of the Bulge from December 17, 1944 to January 24, 1945. In the Bulge, the U.S. troops were in a defensive posture for about two weeks and in an offensive posture for another two weeks. The Bulge ended when the German troops were pushed back to their homeland. The third engagement was really the continuation of the first engagement to defeat the German Troops in the Roer to Rhine River campaign which took approximately 7 days. The detail account of the Roer campaign is provided in the next chapter as told by Lt. Theodore Draper. I was in Paris some 150 miles away.

This was really a remarkable breakthrough.

Lt. Thompson, 1945.

Corp Commander Maj. Gen. Gillem, Jr. and Maj. Gen. Bolling.

CHAPTER 6
ACROSS THE ROER

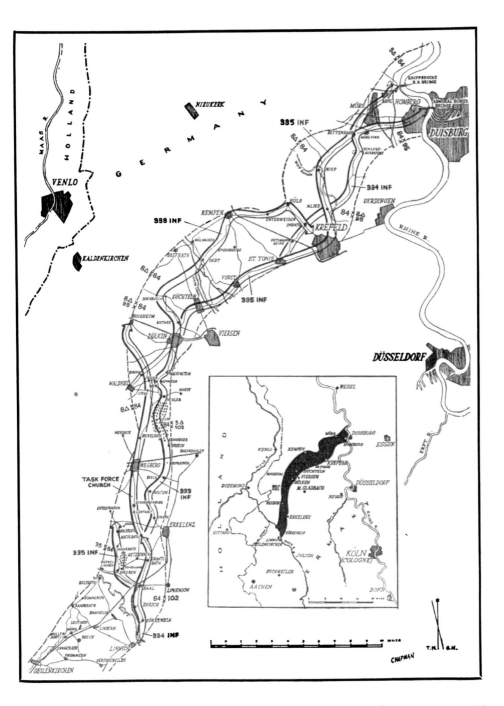

This is an excerpt from Lt. Theodore Draper's <u>The 84th Infantry Division in the Battle of Germany</u>, New York, The Viking Press, 1946.

Now in the public domain.

I n a sense, the crossing was begun with the feints on the two nights before the jump-off. On the night of February 20-21. the concentration was fired from 2 am. to 2:05 am. at the crossing site. A two-hour smoke screen was also laid along the far shore. On the night of February 21-22, this concentration was repeated but the time was changed to 5 a.m. and the place was changed to farther upstream. The smoke screen lasted most of the night to permit the engineers to work near the river bank. As prisoners related later, the crossing was expected on both these nights and the enemy stayed on a very nervous alert but he dropped his guard when it failed to materialize.

On the night of February 22-23, under cover of the smoke screen, the 309th Engineers cleared the routes to the river and marked them with tracing tape. (The third illustration following page 164 shows the details of the Roer crossing.) Six lanes were laid out from the final assembly area to the boat group area, a distance of approximately 700 yards, and 35 lanes from the boat group area to the water's edge, a distance of approximately 200 yards. This job was extremely difficult and dangerous because the enemy was expecting a crossing all night and his artillery was unusually heavy in the whole area. The engineers had to work in the dark under severe fire on one of those minor details that could conceivably determine the fate of the whole undertaking.

It was D-Day, February 23. At 1 a.m., the engineers began to haul the assault boats to the boat assembly areas. They finished at 2 am. The foot bridge equipment was placed in front of the bridge sites between 1 a.m. and 3 a.m. The infantry was also moving. The 334th's 1st Battalion, the first to cross, left its "rear assembly area" in the vicinity of Leilfarth and Würm soon after midnight and marched to the "initial assembly area" in Linnich by 1:30 am. Just outside Linnich, the weapons platoons picked up their machine guns and mortars, which had been carried there the day before to save energy for the crossing. While the men were picking up these heavier guns, the Germans fired a few bursts of machine gun fire at them but the bullets were high. No one stopped working. As they entered the town, a volley of rockets came at them. Everyone smacked into the nearest ditch. Otherwise, the going was smooth.

The 1st Battalion went to the "final assembly area" at 2:45 to meet the engineer guides. They picked up the assault boats, one squad of infantrymen to a boat, one engineer in charge. At 3 sum, they left for the water's edge. From this point on, each boat load was strictly on its own until it reached the next assembly area an the other side of the Roer. "I was thinking about home that morning," Pfc. Leroy Carver, Company C, said. "It was no place for kids there on the river bank. There were too damn many bullets and too much artillery to suit me."

Meanwhile, our artillery and all the supporting weapons, which meant practically everything we had and could commandeer, were thundering away in that tremendous 45-minute preparation. It started at 2:45 am. The effect was a thick. continuous curtain of fire close to the river bank of the far shore. A total of 8400 rounds of field artillery ammunition was expended. The 557th Anti-Aircraft Artillery Battalion fired a total of 272,736 rounds of .50 caliber ammunition, wearing out 125 barrels. The crews of the 771st Tank Battalion supported the crossing and the follow-up for about 15 hours, firing so much ammunition that they often became sick from the fumes in the tanks and had to get out to relieve their nausea. A total of 120,000 rounds were fired by 24 multiple-mount 50 caliber machine guns, and 4000 rounds were sent off by 24 60 mm. mortars in 15 minutes. T/Sgt. George H. Hale, Company C, said the barrage "was so heavy that as we approached the water to man the boats, we were nearly shocked ourselves."

There was one tense moment. At 2:55 a.m., Lt. Eugene R. Giddens, leading the engineer guides, was wounded. Three officers were immediately sent to replace him. Before they could arrive on the scene, all the engineer guides and boat groups were able to meet and find their way. They walked, stumbled, jumped, slid and ran to the water's edge.

The Crossing

At exactly 3:30 a.m.—H-Hour—the artillery barrage was shifted back a few hundred yards. The engineers rushed forward to the footbridge sites with their equipment. The first wave of 35 boats, carrying Companies A and C, 1st Battalion, 334th Infantry, hit the water.

The crossing was unexpectedly easy. "I really don't know whether the enemy fired any shots at us or not," Lt. Richard Hawkins, Company A, said.

"Our own guns going off all around us in support of our crossing drowned out all other sounds." That was one impression. For Company C, T/Sgt. Hale reported: "Going across we received a few 88's and mortars. There were no small arms, except one machine gun which got three men in one of our boats."

Company A came over intact. Company C lost two boats, dragged downstream by the swift current into some burp gun fire. Many boats, however, drifted 75-100 yards downstream in the strong current; this was important because it was impossible to return them in the dark to the west bank to bring across the second crossing battalion. The two companies crossed on a front of approximately 700 yards. The boat trip took about ten minutes. The second wave of boats, bearing Company B and Company D, hit the water at 3:45 am. By 4:05 a.m., the entire 1st Battalion was safely across. The casualties were negligible.

Once across, the troops hit the shore, dropped their rubber life belts, and headed for the railroad track, about 400 yards away, where they had to put together the platoons and companies, split up in the boats for the crossing. Everyone expected the run to the railroad track to be one of the nastiest moments in the job. "What the boys were the most afraid of was the expected mine fields across the river," T/Sgt. Harry L. Peifer, Company A, thought. There were plenty of mines just where we had crossed. The men had a right to worry about them. Lt. Hawkins explained why their fears were not realized: "We went right through a field full of stake mines but all the trip wires attached to the mines had been cut by our artillery and mortars, and not one of the mines exploded in spite of the fact that some of the boys even stumbled over the mines themselves."

The 1st Battalion changed directions as soon as it hit the railroad track. Instead of continuing to go eastward, it struck out for Körrenzig to the north (Map 11). At this time, a momentous decision was made. Resistance was temporarily light because our shelling had driven the Germans into their holes and had taken the fight out of them, but it was clear that sooner or later they would stick their heads out and give us more trouble if they could. The very lack of contact indicated that the enemy was lying low but we could not count on that forever.

Should the 1st Battalion hold up and mop up the bridgehead or should it push on with all possible speed, leaving the mopping up for the 3rd Battalion which was next to cross? It was not a one-sided argument. If the 1st Battalion mopped up, the bridgehead would be safer but the entire drive might have bogged down and the enemy in Körrenzig and farther back might have been given a chance to recover and get set. If the 1st Battalion went ahead without mopping up, an accident or an upset at the bridgehead for the 3rd Battalion might have had disastrous consequences if the follow-up units could not get through in time to assist the 1st.

Either way, risks were unavoidable. The important thing was that we were playing for the highest stakes—a major break-through. We were determined to pass through the crust of German resistance into the soft open spaces in the enemy's rear and develop a momentum which could carry us clear to the Rhine or at least most of the way. To achieve a break-through of such dimensions, only one kind of risk was permissible. It was necessary to race ahead at all costs, to take the fullest advantage of the element of surprise which had already helped us so much in the crossing, to keep the enemy off balance and confused. So the 1st Battalion did not wait to mop up the far bank. It stayed near the bridgehead only long enough to reorganize, and drove for Körrenzig, 1500 yards away, before dawn.

Meanwhile, what was happening at the bridgehead? If the crossing was unexpectedly easy, the footbridges were much more difficult. Though the consequences were never serious, there were some embarrassing moments.

Footbridge No. 1 on the right was almost completed when enemy automatic fire broke out from a stretch of shore that had not been cleaned out. As a result, it could not be anchored on the far bank.

Footbridge No. 2 was completed by 4:10 a.m. but it was immediately knocked out by assault boats that drifted downstream from the 102nd Infantry Division's sector.

Footbridge No. 3 was completed at approximately the same time as Footbridge No. 2 but it was knocked out by a direct hit from enemy artillery which broke the cable.

This fire from the enemy's side was not very heavy, at least not until approximately 5:30 a.m., but in the usual amount of harassing fire, a number of lucky hits were scored. As a result, none of the footbridges were in when the 334th's 3rd Battalion had to cross. At the same time, all the assault boats had not returned from the east bank because so many had drifted downstream. Under fire and in the darkness, it was impossible to recover them in time for the 3rd Battalion. The fate of the first three footbridges and the assault boats necessarily delayed the 3rd Battalion's crossing.

The aggressiveness of the 334th's 1st Battalion is worth some notice. Companies A and C moved into Körrenzig at 6:10 a.m. The 3rd Battalion started to cross the river at 6:45 a.m. In other words, the 1st Battalion had attacked its first town, approximately 2000 yards from the crossing site, before the 3rd Battalion had even begun to cross.

The 3rd Battalion's crossing was slow because it had to resort to a shuttle service. A few boats went over and back for about four hours. Until 10:35 a.m., to bring the whole battalion over. The enemy's artillery was heavier and heavier. While the 3rd Battalion was crossing, lead was falling all over the west bank but the shells were high once the boats hit the water. Some of the boats slammed into the wires stretched across the river by the engineers for the footbridges and the men in them were dumped into the water. Nevertheless, the 3rd Battalion's casualties in the crossing itself were also relatively light.

In the early morning hours of D-Day, then, at least three things were going on at once. The 1st Battalion was striking out to the north. The 3rd Battalion was crossing in relays. The engineers were struggling to put in a footbridge that would stay in. On the whole, we were satisfied but we were not yet breathing freely.

The Bridgehead

For the 1st Battalion, Körrenzig was not as easy as the Roer but it was easier than anyone had expected. In fact, the town was much less troublesome than a marsh and a canal through which they had to wade knee deep to get to it. By the time they were ready to break into the town, everyone was wet, uncomfortable, and angry. Nevertheless, the artillery was still doing a good deal of the work. Just before entering. the infantry called for a special five-minute artillery concentration on Körrenzig. Then Company C took the side of the town nearest the river, Company A the side away from the river. It was still quite dark.

Company C ran into one machine gun which held up the advance temporarily. One rifle grenade and one bazooka round cleared the way. Prisoners were picked up obviously shell-shocked. A German officer gave himself up to Company A in the very first street. At first, he took our men for his own and simply fell into our hands before he knew better. Surprise was still working for us. A few snipers popped out of houses but they were handled on the run. Körrenzig was cleared by 8:30 a.m., about the time half of the 3rd Battalion had succeeded in getting across the Roer. Something which had worried our men was the possibility of German armor in the area. As yet we had no tanks and no anti-tank weapons except bazookas. But no enemy armor was encountered in Körrenzig. This was a major stroke of fortune. Enemy artillery, however, was encountered. As soon as both companies began to dig in, the Germans sent over a heavy barrage which cost us more casualties than the crossing or the town. Nevertheless, the halt at Körrenzig was only two hours. The next objective was Rurich, about 1500 yards slightly northwest. Company A stayed in Körrenzig and Companies B and C drove on. It was 10:30 a.m. By then, the whole 3rd Battalion had crossed the Roer, had disposed of the nests of enemy resistance bypassed at the crossing site, and was hurrying to Körrenzig in the rear of the 1st Battalion.

Rurich was another triumph of surprise. Between Körrenzig and Rurich, only a few scared and scattered enemy posts were met. Rurich itself was attacked at 2:05 p.m. It was cleared in less than a half hour. Rurich was able to put up even less resistance than Körrenzig. Our artillery was waiting impatiently for the word to give Rurich some special attention just before the infantry went in. There was some disappointment when an infantry officer called in to say: "Don't bother. We're in already." But if Rurich was taken without any artillery preparation, the artillery was largely responsible. The tremendous concentrations for the past 12 hours had completely torn up the enemy's communications. The German forces in Rurich knew that we had crossed the Roer only when they saw us in their own town. They had received no warning, no information. No prisoner, officer or enlisted man, knew what Allied unit he was facing.

It had taken us less than 12 hours to obtain a bridgehead about 4000 yards long and 1000 yards deep, though the depth was less important because we were advancing north, not east. The 1st Battalion of the 1034th Volksgrenadiers, 59th Volksgrenadier Division, which outposted the river opposite our crossing, tried to withdraw to a new line of trenches about 800 yards east of Körrenzig. Thus the enemy was maneuvering to meet our attack on the assumption that our direction was straight eastward toward the Rhine. Instead, by turning north from Körrenzig, we met the badly depleted 351st Volksgrenadiers, 183rd Volksgrenadier Division, as well as elements of the 219th Engineer Battalion of the same division. The 183rd had never recovered from its beating in the Geilenltirchen salient and its opposition was not severe.

By the time we had taken Rurich, our whole drive had speeded up. The engineers were reassembled at Footbridge No. 2 and it was successfully completed by 11:30 am. Instead of three footbridges, as planned, only one was actually constructed. The third crossing battalion, the 334th's 2nd Battalion, was, therefore, the first to use the footbridge. The entire regiment was over by 2:50 p.m., soon after the capture of Rurich. It had taken about 12 hours to bring over the first regiment, the 334th Infantry, though this was less important than the fact that the attack was aggressively pushed at all times by as much of the regiment as had managed to cross earlier.

The Battle of Baal

February 23 was one of those long days. Although so much had happened since the jump-off, it was only midafternoon when Rurich was taken. So far the advance was mainly the work of the 334th's 1st Battalion, which received a presidential unit citation for its achievement in the whole Roer-Rhine drive. Fortunately, the 3rd Battalion of the same regiment was not far behind and now it was thrown in to continue the attack, to push the pursuit, as the field order had said, "to the limit of endurance." The next objective was Baal, approximately 2500 yards slightly northeast of Rurich. Ever since its own crossing, the 3rd Battalion had been cleaning out nests of resistance bypassed by the 1st Battalion. At 6:30 p.m., as night was falling, it moved out of Rurich toward Baal. Company K started out on the left, Company L on the right, Company I in reserve. The road passed by a large chateau, then a clearing, then a large patch of woods, another clearing, and finally ran into Baal. About 300 yards from the chateau to the right was a pillbox, skillfully camouflaged as a haystack. The first sign of life in the haystack was a burst of fire.

As soon as the pillbox opened up, Companies L and K drew back to the chateau. Two bazooka teams were sent after the pillbox. Meanwhile, mortars made a bonfire out of the hay, emptying the pillbox and saving the bazookas the trouble. The companies made a fresh start. It was almost dark. Ahead was the patch of woods.

In those woods, for the first time, the enemy showed that the element of surprise was gone and that he was reacting to the attack. Apparently, as our companies were moving out of Rurich toward Baal, an enemy force was moving out of Baal toward Rurich. While we were getting rid of the pillbox, this force, consisting of eight or ten tanks or assault guns and six personnel carriers, was spotted in the woods. Artillery and air were immediately called to deal with them. The enemy's attack was broken before contact on the ground was ever made, another striking example of the assistance our infantry was getting from other arms. Four tanks or assault guns were destroyed, two damaged, and the six personnel carriers knocked out. The remaining tanks or assault guns withdrew toward Baal after dark. The rest of the march from Rurich to Baal was relatively easy. At the outskirts of Baal, the infantry held up while the artillery concentrated on the town for ten minutes. The doughboys moved into another dazed village.

The occupation of Baal was swift. Some burp guns sounded off in the main street but resistance in general was light. By 9:15 p.m., the town was cleared. For the moment, the outlook was bright.

We had estimated that Baal could be taken on D-plus-l, that is, on February 24, so that on this first day we were ahead of schedule. We were also considerably ahead of the divisions on either side so that our flanks were completely exposed, except for the location of our reserves to meet possible counterattacks. The second regiment to cross, the 335th Infantry, started over the footbridge at 4:15 pm. and was completely across before midnight, the 1st Battalion in Rurich, the 2nd Battalion between Rurich and Körrenzig, and the 3rd Battalion in Körrenzig. Our bridgehead, stretching approximately 3½ miles from Linnich to Baal, was occupied by two full infantry regiments before D-Day was finished.

All that day, however, bridges, communications, and contact were still problems. The infantry support bridge was started at 9 am. and opened for traffic by 5:30 pm. But the treadway bridge was strafed by enemy aircraft at 8:30 pm, just as it was ready, and eight floats were hit. It had to be repaired. As a result, no tanks or tank destroyers were able to cross the river on D-Day, leaving the infantry completely without armor support. No wire would stay in across the river under enemy shelling. All efforts by the 334th Infantry to establish contact with the 407th Infantry, 102nd Infantry Division, on the right failed. The 102nd, which crossed below us, also turned north but had farther to go after its wheeling movement to catch up. The 335th's 3rd Battalion was, therefore, thrown in on the right flank of the 334th: Infantry in an effort to make contact with the 407th Infantry in the vicinity of Lovenich.

Perhaps the most critical moment of the first day came at 8:30 p.m. when the treadway bridge was knocked out. In the end, the effect was not serious because our artillery helped to protect the infantry against the enemy's armor. Still, it was a painful moment in an otherwise successful day.

Counterattack at Baal

As far as Baal, we had received no counterattack of large proportions, except for the assault guns and personnel carriers which the combination of air and artillery had routed from the woods between Burich and Baal. On the night of February 28, however, our front was not fully organized because we had moved so fast and because no heavy equipment had moved up with the infantry. The weapons companies had been able to bring across only as much as they could carry by hand, namely, heavy machine guns, 81 mm. mortars, and some mines. The 3rd Battalion was dug in on the northern outskirts of Baal; the 2nd Battalion on the eastern side; the lst Battalion protected the rear or southern side—all 334th Infantry.

Baal was unhealthy from the first. That night, for the first time, the enemy took advantage of the opportunity. At least three German tanks were not hit in the woods and they tried to break out soon after we took over the town. Coming from the direction of Enrich, they entered Baal from the rear and struck Company L. They raked the company CP with point-blank fire. Two GI' s were herding about 30 Germans in one of the streets. The tanks appeared 0n the scene, the prisoners took off, the guards escaped in the darkness and confusion. Then, along the railroad embankment at the far end of Baal, some German machine guns opened fire. Just before the three tanks showed up with headlights blazing, someone in Company L reported they were friendly. Waving and yelling, several men tried to warn the tanks away from the machine gun fire. The enemy tankers let them have an extra burst of lead in return. Raking the buildings all the way, the tanks drove out of Baal to Granterath. This was merely an incident, not the enemy's main effort which came somewhat later, but it helped to give our men the nervous feeling that anything could happen in Baal that night. Anything almost did.

Just before midnight, at 11:40 p.m., still February 23, three enemy battalions and three assault guns launched a counterattack. The 2nd Battalion of the 343rd Volksgrenadiers, 183rd Volksgrenadier Division, moved southeast from Doveren. The 176th Fusilier Battalion, 176th Volksgrenadier Division, moved south from Hetzerath. The 2nd Battalion, 330th Volksgrenadiers, 183rd Volksgrenadier Division, attempted to outflank us on the right from Granterath. Artillery fire stopped the center prong from Hetzerath but the other two attacks from the flanks struck Company L and Company K.

Company L's 2nd Platoon was trying to defend a vital underpass and road junction on the road to Granterath from a battered building. One German unit succeeded in reaching the 30-foot railroad embankment and underpass. Machine guns and rifles opened up on the 2nd Platoon.

"Enemy bullets began pounding the rear of the building," Lt. William

Nelson said. "Germans seemed to be everywhere but in the dark they could not be spotted. Machine gun and BAR flre held the attackers back but our ammunition ran low. The situation became so critical that there was nothing left to do but to call down artillery on that very spot. I had no radio communications so I sent runners to the company CP but they never got there. Lucky for us, the company commander had received word from somewhere else that there was trouble and he called for artillery on the underpass. For an hour the underpass was shelled and my platoon sweated it out in our house which was only 25 yards away."

This artillery treatment saved the 2nd Platoon. All through the night our men could hear the Germans near the underpass crying out, begging for the shelling to be lifted. One German-speaking GI yelled at them to surrender. In small groups, they charged across the road to give themselves up. Some dragged or carried wounded. In the end, about 25 prisoners were jammed in the already crowded cellar of the house. They claimed that they were the only ones left of the 200 or more men who had started the attack from Granterath. Then the artillery was lifted.

Company L's 1st Platoon had a similar experience. First the second squad was surrounded. The Germans called on them to surrender. The BAR man opened up and managed to cover the squad's escape. The third squad was less fortunate. It was surrounded in a house, the Germans told them to give up, a well-placed hand grenade talked back. German bazookas forced them to jump upstairs. They could not see what was going on outside but they kept flinging out hand grenades and firing rifles to discourage an assault on the house. For awhile, there was a stalemate; the enemy could not get into the house and they could not get out. Finally, artillery arrived. When the shells began to remove the top floor, the squad made a hasty return to the bottom floor. It was nerve-racking but the Germans were forced to leave.

Company K was also protecting an overpass, this one on the road to Doveren. The platoons were holding houses on both sides of the road. When the enemy attack came, artillery was requested. The story was virtually the same. "Another request came in for artillery closer to our positions," 1st Sgt. Paul Long said. "It was already falling within 75 feet of us. This time the artillery actually fell in the street between the houses in which the platoons had their positions. Then one of our boys spotted a German tank firing at us from across the street. We thought our time was up and we burned all the papers we had on us. But our artillery fire became so hot that the tank withdrew. The artillery also proved too much for the German infantry and the whole attack fizzled out."

The battle of Baal ended strangely. Just before dawn, February 24, three German tanks and some infantry support came down the road from Granterath at Company L's 2nd Platoon, which had had barely enough time to recover from its experiences earlier that night. The enemy force stopped outside the underpass, not more than 500 yards from the platoon, which had used up all its machine gun ammunition and all its grenades. Only one bazooka round was left. The tanks sat there for an hour. Our men watched them tensely, wondering what we could do this time to hold them off if they drove in. But apparently the German tankers were not sure of themselves either. As the dim light of morning spread out, the German tanks backed away.

Also connected with the battle of Baal was an attempt later that morning, at about 8 a.m., February 24, to retake Rurich in order to cut off our forces in Baal. The 5th and 7th Companies of the 330th Volksgrenadiers, 183rd Volksgrenadier Division, tried to slip in between Baal and Lovenich but walked into the fire of the 335th's 3rd Battalion. The battalion opened up when the German column was only 100 yards away. Apparently the enemy's officers abandoned their men. The demoralization was sudden and complete.

"The enemy was in a perfect position for us to shoot at him," T/ Sgt. Harold E. Baker, Company K, said. "They stumbled upon us without knowing we were there, a fact that was later confirmed by some prisoners. We continued firing everything we had for about two hours. The artillery joined in. Finally, Pfc. Edward J. Serris calmly left his foxhole, walked to the enemy positions, and brought in 15 prisoners. From then on, others continued to bring in prisoners. At about 4 o'clock, we were ordered to advance 1000 yards, which carried us right through the enemy's foxholes. We found the German positions full of casualties and others stunned by the terrific shelling."

The action was over before dusk, February 24, and so was the battle of Baal. The 334th's 3rd Battalion also received a presidential unit citation for its part in the Roer-Rhine advance.

On the morning of D-plus-1, February 24, then, the combination of infantry and artillery had demonstrated that our bridgehead was solid. The treadway bridge was also put in to stay in. It was opened at 11:20 am. A few minutes earlier, two ME 262's, German twin engine jet planes, came over to bomb and strafe the bridge sites. The gunners of Battery C, 557th AAA (AW) Battalion, hit the first one on its first trip over. It tumbled down. The second plane came in to bomb the bridge. One of its bombs was hit in mid-air and exploded. The gunners let go at the plane and struck it, too. It tried to get away but soon crashed near by. The two planes were the first of this type shot down by the XIII Corps.

The first tanks rolled across the treadway bridge almost immediately. Company A, 771st Tank Battalion, crossed the Roer at noon and arrived in Baal two hours later in time to assist in mopping up the town of the last snipers and stragglers. Company C and Company B followed in that order and the entire tank battalion was over by 11 p.m. that same day. It should be noted that the infantry did not have any armor support across the river for almost 36 hours.

Thus far our infantry advance had been achieved solely by the 334th Infantry, the first to cross. It was now the turn of the 335th Infantry, the second to cross, to widen and deepen the penetration.

At 9 a.m., February 24, just as Baal was quieting down, the 335th's 1st Battalion moved up from Rurich to Baal in order to pass through the 334th in Baal and continue the attack. As so often happens in such a swift advance, pockets of resistance have to be cleaned up by the follow-up units for some time and the "rear" may be just as jumpy as the "front." The 335th's 1st Battalion had to fight its way to Baal, especially in the woods between Burich and Baal, which had given us so much trouble the day before. Its objective was Doveren, about 2500 yards northwest of Baal, and Doverhahn, a little village on the eastern outskirts of Doveren.

Even to get out of Baal, the 1st Battalion had to fight hard. About 200 yards north of Baal, just beyond the railroad along the Baal-Doveren road, it ran into stiff opposition from enemy small arms and machine gun fire. It was midday before the dug-in Germans were cleaned out. As a result, the 335th's 2nd Battalion was committed on the 1st Battalion's left flank. The 2nd was Ordered to move through Rurich to the northwest, cutting across country to strike directly at Doveren. The 2nd also hit resistance almost immediately from entrenched enemy infantry along the Brachelen-Baal railroad. Instead of holding up, however, it swung over to the right as far as the western edge of Baal and bypassed the whole thing.

While the 1st Battalion was held up outside Baal, word was received that tank support was coming. At 2:30 p.m., the 771st's Company C arrived. It immediately launched an attack, using its entire complement of tanks. The 76's fired away over the heads of our own infantry. Both tanks and infantry broke through. In Doveren, the tanks again played a leading role. At first the command tank and two other tanks were cut off in the center of the town. When the infantry was delayed, it was necessary to dismount the crews to protect the tanks. By nightfall, the infantry had control of the situation and the tanks were freed to take up positions to the north to guard against counterattacks. Doverhahn was seized by Company C's tanks without infantry support. Meanwhile, the 335th's 2nd Battalion was marching toward Doveren, following the railroad from Baal. It arrived shortly after nightfall, not too late to get into the scrap. The town was burning, snipers were still active, and a counterattack was momentarily awaited.

That night, D~plus-1, February 24, our bridgehead extended from Linnich to Doveren, approximately 4 miles in length. We had driven a wedge into the German positions extending from the eastern edge of Hückelhoven, through Doveren, Doverhahn, and Baal, approximately 8 miles in width. Our flanks were still wide open. The 102nd Infantry Division on our right was held up about 3000 yards behind us and the 35th Infantry Division on our left had not yet jumped off to take Hilfarth and cross the river in its zone. The problems of the crossing, however, were behind us and we were able to turn our full attention to the problem of exploiting our success to the "limit of endurance." We were beginning to look for the right moment to burst out in a full-scale break-through.

D-plus-2

From D-plus-2 on, we had two regiments abreast in the corridor that we were driving toward the north, the 334th Infantry on the east, the 335th Infantry on the west. The regimental picture, however, was more complex than usual. The 338rd's 1st Battalion was attached to the 335th Infantry and the 335th's 3rd Battalion was attached to the 834th Infantry.

Whatever problems we still faced, the enemy was obviously in a much more difficult position. His communications were still so disrupted that surprise remained an important factor on our side. On the night of February 24-25, we received the most striking evidence of the enemy's complete bafflement. At 11 p.m., February 24, our D-plus-1-Day, the 2nd Company, 343rd Infantry, was ordered to move from Hilfarth to take up a defensive position in Doveren. This unit arrived on the scene the next day only to find that Doveren was no longer in German hands. Instead of going into Doveren, it merely organized a defensive position north of the town. One reason Doveren was taken by us without much more trouble was this inability of the German command to keep up with the situation. The system of sending reserve forces to defend threatened points did not work out because these points were frequently not merely threatened—they were captured—by the time the units were able to come within striking distance. Then the units, which had expected to defend, had to attack, or, more likely, would find themselves attacked before they could react to the new situation.

In the case of Doveren, the 2nd Company, 343rd Infantry, did not launch the counterattack at all. The 1st Battalion, 351st Volksgrenadiers, 183rd Volksgradier Division, passed through it at about 2:80 a.m. on the morning of February 25 to do the fighting. The enemy's attack was vigorous but it was too little and too late. We already had two full infantry battalions and one full tank company in Doveren. The counterattack was thrown back by an unusually neat triple play which showed the high degree of co-ordination which our infantry-tank-artillery forces had reached.

It was the practice of the 771st Tank Battalion to send one staff officer with a radio to the artillery battalion in direct support of the infantry regiment with which one of the tank companies was working. In this case, the 335th Infantry and the 771st's Company C were involved. This liaison officer stayed in the fire direction center to work in the closest relationship with the artillery. In this way, each tank became a forward observer for the artillery and each tanker could adjust the artillery's fire.

When the 1st Battalion, 351st Volksgrenadiers, hit Doveren, Company C's tanks had radio communication with the infantry but the artillery did not. On the other hand, the tanks could get through to their liaison officer in the fire direction center. For approximately four hours, Captain B. C. Mills of Company C directed artillery fire on the enemy's counterattack and eventually broke it up. By daybreak, Doveren was safe from everything but the enemy's artillery.

Our last difficulty with the bridges also came in the early morning hours of D-plus-2. At 2:30 a.m., February 25, both the infantry support bridge and the headway bridge were hit by shell fire. The infantry support bridge had to be repaired before it could be used again but the treadway bridge could still handle 2 1/2-ton trucks without trailers. Soon after, at 4 a.m., the Bailey bridge at Korrenzig was completed so that the heaviest vehicles could cross the river for the first time. At 5:45 am, another burst of enemy shell-fire struck seven pontoons of the treadway bridge and closed it temporarily. The treadway bridge was repaired by 10:30 a.m., the infantry support bridge by 2 p.m. That was the end of our bridge troubles.

Meanwhile, both the 334th Infantry and the 335th Infantry pushed on, the former from Baal, the latter from Doveren. So much materiel was across that the temporary holdup at the bridges was no handicap. At 9:30 a.m., the 334th's 3rd Battalion jumped off for Granterath, approximately 1000 yards northeast of Baal. At the same time, the 834th's 1st Battalion struck out for Hetzerath, an equal distance due north. At 10 a.m., the 335th's 2nd Battalion pushed on to Houverath, approximately 2000 yards north of Doveren.

The 334th's 3rd Battalion met some resistance from enemy machine guns, a self-propelled gun, and a Mark V tank midway between Baal and Granterath. The 771st's Company A was called up and laid down a base of fire which enabled the infantry to move forward again. Our tanks knocked out a half-track, two self-propelled guns, and the Mark V tank. Company I cleaned out the northern half of Granterath, Company K the southern half. The town was cleared by 2:15 p.m. Infantry resistance inside was light.

Hetzerath was taken by the 334th's 1st Battalion without tank support. Company A was held up in some mods on the way by snipers who, for a change, were remarkably accurate. One man was actually shot in the jaw lying on the ground. But the 334th's 2nd Battalion was moving up in the same general direction and enabled Company A to go on. Company C found an enemy trench which protected it most of the way. About 150 yards from Hetzerath, five enemy machine guns were spotted. All were manned. At our approach, four crews abandoned their guns, the fifth was persuaded by a fling of "marching fire." Once inside, Hetzerath was mopped up by 3:20 p.m.

The story of Houverath was told by Captain Francis K. Price, S-3 of the 335th's 2nd Battalion: "1 like to tell myself that it was a perfect operation, the sort of thing they dream of at Fort Benning. We moved northeast from Doveren, Company E with a platoon of heavy machine guns from Company H and Company C of the 771st Tank Battalion. Ahead of us was as neat a set of trench works, anti-tank ditches, and obstacles as I have seen. The doughboys double timed, firing as they ran, while from their flanks the heavy machine guns covered them and over their heads the tanks were spitting lead from their machine guns and 76's. The Jerries in the trenches came out with their hands up and we waved them to the rear."

In front of Houverath was a woods. "As we burst through the woods, a column of six Mark IV tanks was sighted moving down the road from Matzerath to Hetzerath towards the 334th. Captain Mills of the 771st called on the radio and we made up our minds at once. Two platoons of his company swung off to the right and blazed away at this threat to our flank. I ordered one platoon of Company E to hold fast and seal off that flank. But we were moving too fast to be sidetracked from our main effort. The remainder of Company E and the other platoon of tanks took off for Houverath itself. The 76's on the tanks smashed the town to rubble before our very eyes and the doughboys ran right into it." From the woods to the occupation of Houverath was a matter of less than 40 minutes.

Thus on this third day of our drive, we began to detect signs of greatly increasing disintegration in the enemy's ranks. Volkssturm elements were encountered for the first time but were committed as replacements for the 183rd Volksgrenadier Division, not as a unit. This division seemed on the verge of complete disintegration as prisoners from every one of its regiments increased. Many were sent into the line so frantically that they did not know to what company they belonged. Confusion was gradually but unmistakably setting in.

There were strong indications that the enemy's organized defense extended only as far as Baal and Doveren. At Baal, also, we apparently forced him to displace an important portion of his artillery. He was handicapped, therefore, for two or three days before he could bring his guns into new positions. In any case, we had three days of hard fighting. After D-plus-2, there was a distinct change.

CHAPTER 7
PASS TO PARIS

I now share my personal experience in this chapter. The reason will be obvious that it was more than a routine of my duties as an executive officer for E company, 334th infantry. After Lt. Thompson, commander of the company, crossed the Roer River on a foot walk pontoon bridge with his Company on February 23, 1945, we all had advanced to a wooded area outside of the town of Baal, Germany. The Company occupied German communication trenches and remained there because of German troop activity around our position. I was at the extreme end of the trench, guarding the area behind the company. At one point, I spoke to Lt. Thompson and get the latest information. I found a group of the company soldiers with Lt. Thompson in a tiny hutment or structure above the trench level and commented that they should disperse along with the company SCR radio operator carrying a radio with a long antenna.

After I returned to my rear position, I discovered that one of our replacement officers from Alaska was killed on the very spot that I had visited. Of course, Lt. Thompson and the others were not in harm's way. On that day, February 25, 1945 (D-Day+2), I received orders to go on a Paris pass for three days. I did not realize at the time that perhaps some general had ordered it. E company was just south of the German town of Baal, and I missed moving out to make the breakthrough with the 334th infantry Regiment in the initial formation of the Task Force Church, named after our 84th division, assistant commander, Brig. Gen. John Church.

I hurried back to the west side of the Roer River very early in the day. There were no troops around the river footbridge and I was alone to report to the regimental headquarters. Somehow, I was taken back to the town of Palenberg where I could shower and dress in my uniform. My officers dress uniform was in a storage area and not available, so I was furnished with a battlefield uniform. The next morning February 26, 1945, I was with other combatants left by a 2 ½ ton truck to be headed for Paris. It took us 14 hours to get there since the roads and travel were slow. When we arrived in Paris, we were taken to the Grand Hotel on the Opera, a five-star hotel. It was a beautiful place. I was never in my life in a hotel except one in New Orleans, Louisiana where Lt. Thompson and I shared a sweltering room with no windows in the middle of a summer day in 1944. It was the only room available in town.

Upon my arrival in Paris, I felt feverish stayed around the hotel enjoying the donuts and coffee made available there. The hotel dining room had huge fancy tables. However, the food was Army grade since the Army had taken over the whole hotel for R&R (rest and recreation). It was still very special compared to the rations or the occasional hot meal our cooks prepared for us in theater. The few things that I recall during my short time in Paris were the taxi tours of the city and museum visits. I did, however, walk some of their famous streets. I never went up the Eiffel tower though. Sleeping in a big, luxurious bed was like heaven. As a matter of fact, the whole time in Paris seemed unreal, but it was over too soon. Of course, my two and a half ton truck transportation was ready for me to return back to the Roer River area in Germany. I was as surprised as the Germans to learn that in the three days that I was gone, Task Force Church was formed (February 26th/D-Day+3) and made the breakthrough without me. The Task Force Church went 10 miles on the first day of the breakthrough, D-Day+5.

This is a good time to tell you that I returned to E Company by dropping off one of the trucks and loading onto another 2 1/2 ton truck. E Company was a major part of Task Force Church. The 334th infantry was also a large part of this task force which was motorized and ready to make another breakthrough to Suchteln and Mors on March 2 – 4, 1945. It was exhilarating to be part of this great machine where the sense of power and elation was common across my men. This gave us momentum and motivation to keep pushing forward to the ultimate objective. The last phase, March 4 -5, took the towns of Mors and Homberg. This was D-Day+10.

Troops of the 84th division spent the rest of the month in and around the town of Homberg on the Rhine River. It was like an extended Paris pass again for me with all my troops around me. I must say that we were about 30 days ahead of schedule. I am sure that many American lives were saved, as well as enemy lives, because of our rapid advance from the Roer River to the Rhine River. After Homberg, who needs a Paris pass?

Task Force Church, Feb. 26 1945.

Hotel Grande, Paris, Feb. 25 1945.

CHAPTER 8
THE BREAKTHROUGH

This is an excerpt from Lt. Theodore Draper's <u>The 84th Infantry Division in the Battle of Germany</u>, New York, The Viking Press, 1946.

The breakthrough is probably the most rewarding achievement of modern ground warfare. It has been made possible by the speed and firepower of modern weapons and equipment. It is an unmistakable demonstration that those weapons have been exploited to the fullest. The German triumph in the west in 1940 was decided by the breakthrough from Sedan to Abbeville. The Allies turned the tables in 1944 by the breakthrough from Normandy to the German border. Every one of the decisive victories in the war, on both western and eastern fronts, has involved in some form, a breakthrough.

The reason is paradoxical. In modern warfare, both sides are usually able to mass so much force that a knockdown, drag-out fight may end without a real victor. It may be so exhausting that both sides have to give themselves a period of recuperation before they can go at each other again. The margin of victory in a drawn-out, close-in struggle is generally so small that it is not worth the gigantic effort which it demands. A breakthrough is just the opposite of such a battle of attrition. It achieves the maximum results at a minimum cost. It makes it possible to cover the most ground in the shortest time, bring in the most prisoners, suffer the least casualties, use up the smallest amount of material, and mark off one map after another. In an encirclement an enemy force can be crushed but a tremendous amount of manpower may be necessary to close all the escape routes and an immense pressure may be applied slowly and painfully as the trapped forces try vainly to break out. In a breakthrough, the relatively small forces of the leading elements may do nine-tenths of the fighting. They have not overwhelmed the enemy but they have done something much cheaper and much more effective. They have overawed him.

Our advance to Houverath, Hetzerath, and Granterath on February 25 was so convincing that it put the possibility of a breakthrough on the order of the day. A major breakthrough was one of the few important military operations which the 84th had not yet experienced. After the weeks of slugging in the Siegfried Line and the weeks of suffering in the Ardennes, it had a special meaning for us. It was the "pay off." To a soldier who has had to fidget for every miserable yard in mud and snow, a fast ride on firm roads, peeling off mile after mile, rarely firing a shot, passing thousands of prisoners, is a joy which seems too perfect for this imperfect world.

D-Day+3

On February 26, the fourth day, we began to do something to achieve a breakthrough. It was a day of preparation but there was no letup in the fighting. Before we could lash out into the open, we continued to lengthen and broaden our corridor for another 24 hours. This time the 335th's 3rd Battalion took the lead on the left flank. Company I and a platoon of tanks went for Golkrath, K Company and another tank platoon for Hoven (Map 11). Jumping off from Houverath, I Company was harassed by enemy artillery and mortars all the way. Despite the shelling, the company reported that it crossed the 1,200 yards of open ground to Golkrath in six minutes. Inside the town, resistance was light. Golkrath was cleared by noon. Hoven was cleared by Company K 25 minutes later. Later that afternoon, L Company went out of Colkrath to cut the main Erkelenz-Gerderhahn road. The main objective on February 26 of the 102nd Infantry Division on our right Bank was Erkelenz. By cutting the road, we helped to isolate Erkelenz.

On the 334th Infantry's side of the corridor, the 2nd Battalion and the 771st's Company A went forward at noon to get Matzerath. No opposition was encountered, but Matzerath will always mean two things to the men who went into it. It was the first town which we overran so quickly that the civilian population was still intact. It was the first town in which beer was found. The era of deserted villages was over. If anything was still necessary to indicate that a breakthrough was imminent, this was it. The Erkelenz-Gerderhahn road was also cut in the 334th's sector.

A staff meeting was held on the evening of D-Day+3, February 26, to decide how to exploit the enemy's obvious disorganization to the utmost. General Bolling had been playing with the idea for so long that only the details had to be fitted in. The outcome of this meeting was not only a plan but an attitude. Gone were the days when we set our objectives in terms of yards, we were thinking in miles. Gone were the days when attacks were based on companies, battalions, or even regiments. We were thinking in "task forces," in a combination of all arms, a division in miniature.

The modern infantry division has much more than infantry in it and, to that extent, the name may be misleading. Although the infantry is still its basis, every other arm is represented—even the air force in the form of observation planes and an air liaison officer. It is, therefore, not necessary to go outside an infantry division to put together a force which for speed, power, and flexibility may be the equal of any. Such a force was our aim to achieve the breakthrough.

The result was Task Force Church. It was commanded by the Assistant Division Commander, General Church. It was the first fully motorized task force of the division. Task Force Church was made up of a tank battalion, an infantry regiment, an artillery battalion, an anti-aircraft battery, a tank destroyer company, an engineer company, a medical company, the reconnaissance troop, a detachment of military police, and a signal detachment. It was strong enough to slash through any possible opposition, fast enough to cover the maximum ground in the shortest time, self-sufficient enough to hold out alone if the rest of the division was held up, flexible enough to attack, defend, ride, walk, smash through, or slip through.

Task Force Church moved out in the following formation:

771st Tank Battalion (Company A, 334th Infantry, riding on the leading tanks)

1st Battalion, 334th Infantry (less Company A), motorized

Command Group, Task Force Church

Cannon Company, 334th Infantry

84th Reconnaissance Troop (—) (Remainder of Troop cori-ducted reconnaissance to flanks)

Company B, 309th Engineer (C) Battalion

326th FA Battalion

Battery D, 557th AAA (AW) Battalion

3rd Battalion, 334th Infantry, motorized

Command Group, 334th Infantry

Company A, 637th TD Battalion, reinforced

Special Units, 334th Infantry

Company B, 309th Medical Battalion

2nd Battalion, 334th Infantry

The mission of Task Force Church was published in a Letter of Instruction, issued at 6 p.m., February 26, and preparations were made the rest of the night to put it into effect. The jump-off was made from Matzevath. The first objective was Wegberg, approximately 5 miles away. The second objective was Waldniel, approximately 10 miles away. After Waldniel, the

Rhine was the limit. The 333rd Infantry and the 335th Infantry were told to get ready to follow up by motor on two hours' notice to mop up.

It should be noted that the 334th Infantry in Task Force Church had made the original crossing, had smashed through the crust as far as Baal, and had been fighting for four days with no more than two or three hours sleep a day. Throughout this phase of the operation, our flanks were still open. To have waited for safe flanks, however, would have given the enemy a chance to catch his second wind. In the end, it was safer to drive forward to take advantage of the enemy's distress than to stop for a rest or for more flank protection. There were risks. There always were. But Task Force Church was such a coordinated concentration of force that the risks were minimized.

D-Day+4

At 6:50 a.m. on February 27, the big guns began to pound away. The racket, as usual, was terrific. The first target was the village of Lentholt on the other side of the Erkelenz road. The concentration lasted ten minutes. Then Task Force Church took off. It was 7 am. The front lines were crossed just north of Hoven. The tanks, doughhoys holding on grimly to anything that stuck out of the frames, went first. The entire column stretched out for miles. It was gray and misty.

The first stop of Task Force Church was Wegberg. It was approximately 8:30 a.m. Compared to our pace the first four days, this advance—5 miles in an hour and a half—was already a breakthrough. In some towns the tanks moved at a speed of 25 miles per hour. At the northern outskirts of Wegberg, however, a railroad underpass was skillfully demolished. B Cornpany's tanks were permitted to go through, the underpass was blown, the debris blocked the main road. Engineers were rushed forward to clear the way but it was almost noon before the advance was resumed. At about 3 pm, it was decided to commit the entire 1st Battalion, 334th Infantry, against the threat which amounted to four anti-tank guns and five assault guns. Meanwhile, the "rear" areas of the column were also warm. An experience of General Church showed how fluid the situation could be 3-4 miles behind the tank spearhead.

When the column was held up near Steeg, General Church decided to go up there to see for himself. His party was made up of three jeeps, his own, an I, and R jeep, and a third, some distance behind, with two newspaper correspondents. About 400 yards north of Wegberg a burst of fire suddenly came from the I and R jeep. A German soldier was firing back 10 feet away from a ditch. About 300 yards farther, eight more were dug in along theroad. Two jeeps raced past, everyone shooting, hoping this was an isolated, die-hard group of Germans. When still more enemy riflemen were encountered, however, it was decided to go back because it was impossible to tell how many more were waiting along the road. Meanwhile, the correspondents had turned back at the first sign of trouble to bring help.

By turning around, General Church's jeep became the leading vehicle. Halfway through the first pocket of resistance, the two jeeps were caught in heavy fire from the other side of the road. 01: the way up, they had not noticed that both sides of the road were alive with Germans. General

Church's car was hit and reeled. The driver, T/5 Kyser Crockett, said: "I've lost my arm," as he slumped in his seat, trying to keep his foot on the accelerator. The general's aide, Lt. Norman D. Dobie, leaned over from the back seat and steered the jeep through the fire. General Church's automatic blazed away. had successfully passed the gauntlet did Lt. Dobie notice that General Church's face and clothes were streaked with blood. A doctor examined General Church in the temporary headquarters at the southern edge of Wegberg and found that fragments had hit him below the eyebrow, around the knee, and the most serious one in the ankle. T/5 Crocket suffered a complex fracture of the forearm. General Church's experience did not prevent him from moving about and he finished the entire drive to the Rhine.

The fight against the anti-tank guns took up the rest of the day. When darkness set in and the movement of our armor was restricted, the infantry organized a defense line south of Steeg. The first day of Task Force Church was finished.

What was our achievement? On February 27, the 84th Infantry Division led the Allied armies in the drive to the Rhine. Its breakthrough was the first of its kind by any division, armored or infantry, in the battle of Germany. By running away with the enemy, we had also run away from our friends. flanks that day were simply forgotten. On February 27, the 102nd Infantry Division and the 5th Armored Division on our right had seized

Rheindahlen, approximately 5 miles behind us. The 35th Infantry Division on our left had taken Gerderhahn, approximately 7 miles behind us.

After the deep penetration of Task Force Church, the 335th Infantry on the left and the 333rd Infantry on the right proceeded to mop up scattered enemy units, including the 4th Battalion, 1176th FA Regiment (150 mm Howitzers), and a searchlight battery, both complete with equipment intact. In the 9-mile sweep, 54 towns and villages were overrun. The enemy's casualties for the day were estimated at 100 killed, 50 wounded, and 1249 prisoners—completely reversing the ordinary proportions of casualties. The enemy's equipment captured, damaged, or destroyed amounted to 12 FA guns, 8 88 mm. AA/AT guns, 2 assault guns, 17 motor vehicles, and 15 horse-drawn wagons. At Beeck, southeast of Wegberg, one of the most important enemy maps ever to fall into Allied hands while its information was still current was discovered. A member of the wire section of the 327th FA Battalion, PTC. B. O. Davis, found the map, showing the exact location of all German units on the western front, in the headquarters of the 12th SS Corps which was abandoned so hastily that even such maps were left behind. The map was forwarded to SHAEF headquarters in Paris in a few hours.

The human aspects of a major breakthrough have a special interest, especially the prisoners and the civilian population. Our total bag of prisoners in the Siegfried Line in five weeks of continuous fighting was 1548. Our total bag of prisoners in the Ardennes in four weeks of continuous fighting was 1503. In a single day, February 27, we took in 1249. Not that any particular effort was made to gather in prisoners during the breakthrough. None was necessary. Hordes simply decided that the war was over for them and started marching in column to the rear. Most of these pessimistic characters were not fighting men. They were clerks, shoemakers, tailors, blacksmiths, butchers. Some were just banded rifles and told to defend a ditch which they never found. Others were caught as we overran rear echelons. Artillerymen were also unusually numerous. Replacement units were captured intact before they could turn themselves into combat units. In fact, cohesive units with definite sectors were unknown. The remnants seemed to amount to groups of men thrown together wherever they could be found. It was almost useless to pump prisoners for information. They were confused, stunned, ignorant. All they knew was that we were not supposed to be where we were. That was one reason so little fight was put up. They were demoralized, and demoralized soldiers do not fight.

Full credit for the first breakthrough in Germany was given to the 84th in the entire American press the next day. Most of the reports played up the fact that an infantry division, rather than an armored division, had slashed through first, though some neglected to mention that tanks had led the way for us, too. The Associated Press said that "the German lines fell apart yesterday under a 9 mile thrust by motorized infantry of the Eighty-fourth Division." The New York Times noted that "it was not even an armored spearhead that made the greatest gain of the day on the Ninth

Army front but an infantry column of the Eighty-fourth Division." The Army's own Stars and Stripes wrote that "in one sector of what was modestly called a *fluid* front in official reports, the 84th's 334th had even outrun the tanks." Actually, the 84th's tanks outran all the other tanks.

D-Day+5

Company C, its strength reduced to 125 men, led off for the 334th's 2ndBattalion. It started out from a group of cottages near Wegberg known as a "model village." To reach the road to Berg, it was necessary to cross 300 yards of open field. Near the highway, four enemy machine guns opened up. One was off to the right of the main road, the other three behind a slope to the front. Lt. Harold L. Howdieshell, whose battlefield commission was still very strange and new, had both his scouts with him, about 25 yards ahead of the company. He spotted the machine gun that was hitting the 1st Platoon. It was all to the right. He pushed his scouts into the ditch beside the road and pegged four hand grenades at the gun. It was not heard from again. Just as he was about to pull the pin from a fifth grenade, another machine gun cut loose at him. He died instantly.

The second machine gun was located. It was firing from a low-slung, one-story building. A stream of bullets forced the 1st Platoon to hug the ground. Gradually, about half the platoon managed to crawl up to a sugar beet mound which provided some protection. Lt. Jack F. Schaper crawled around the mound to observe the position of the gun. Just as his head was far enough out to get a view, he was hit, a head wound. The same gun scored twice more.

The company commander, Captain Charles E. Hiatt, decided to send his 2nd Platoon on a flanking movement through a patch of woods and knock out the gun from the left side. This platoon picked up 15 prisoners in the woods, each one an officer or noncom. The house was rushed and the second machine gun was eliminated. A high German officer was found at the helm of a double-barreled gun. From that building, the German defense was sized up. The second gun had covered the crest of the slope behind which the Germans were dug in. It was a perfect reverse slope defense. Machine gun fire covered every avenue of approach but, with two guns out, it was possible to storm the crest of the slope and land on the Germans dug in behind.

At first, progress was slow and hard. One enemy machine gun continued to cut all around Company C. Burp guns and small arms fire added to the danger. They hugged their side of the slope, waiting for the fire to quiet down. Everyone took a turn, raised himself up for a moment, let go with a slug, snapped back to the ground for safety. Suddenly someone said: "To hell with this! Let's rush 'em!" They charged up the crest of the slope, bayonets fixed. They sprang into the trenches, arms, bayonets, and hand grenades flying. The Germans were paratroopers and fought back gamely. Only two were left to be captured when it was all over.

And so, in the middle of the night, at 1:30 a.m., March 1, the column began to move again. The attack on Boisheim was spearheaded by the 334th's 3rd Battalion and the 771st's A Company. It was one of the easiest and quickest victories in our experience. The surprise was absolute. About

300 yards out of Boisheim, K Company, in the lead, stopped to take care of two anti-tank guns. The information was given to them by a child at a farmhouse. The guns were seized without protest. Boisheim itself was asleep. In order to take prisoners, GI's had to raid houses on a grand scale. Boisheim produced more prisoners in bed than any other place in the drive. By 6:30 a.m., March 1, Boisheim was ours. Yet, the approaches to Boisheim were covered by anti-tank guns with excellent fields of fire. These weapons might have given us as much trouble as the guns at the approaches to Waldniel but that night they were not even manned.

Boisheim is a convenient midway point to look back at the entire drive. In six days, the 84th Infantry Division had advanced 20 miles from the Roer. Two-thirds of that distance was covered in the last two days. In this period. 2876 prisoners were captured. At the same time, the total of prisoners of the XIII Corps was 6444 and it was 11,624 for the Ninth Army. The 84th was responsible, therefore, for 44 per cent of the Corps' total and 24 per cent of the Army's total.

In retrospect, the crossing seems remarkably easy, the pursuit remarkably successful, the enemy's disintegration remarkably advanced. If so, the credit must go to the painstaking planning, preparation, and training for every move; the coordination of all arms, especially the infantry, armor, artillery, and engineers; and the extraordinary demands which our men made on themselves in the chase. If the enemy had been permitted to reorganize his positions even once, there might have been a different story.

At the Rhine

Boisheim was one of the turning points in the drive to the Rhine. From the Roer to Boisheim, we were traveling northward instead of eastward. The enemy was fooled because we seemed to be going away from the Rhine, our obvious objective, and his disposition of troops and defenses were primarily aimed to defend the Rhine against a drive to the east. This northward direction, however, enabled us to break out of the area of the enemy's prepared defenses in a relatively short time and to strike out into relatively open country in which armor was most effective.

We had fine roads to roll on. We were cutting across corps and even armies, always at the weakest points, so that by the time the element of surprise was lost in one zone we were able to take advantage of it in another.

When Boisheirn was reached, it was clear that a change of direction was indicated in order to confuse the enemy once more. After 20 miles of the northward push, it was safe to assume that the Germans had adjusted themselves to the threat from that direction. At Boisheim, therefore, the drive was suddenly twisted to the east. There was reason to suspect that the enemy might be surprised again by the change in direction and that he would again permit us to maneuver behind his lines. The great advantage of this strategy was that it forced the enemy to fight on our terms, not us on his. It was a complete reversal of the situation in the Siegfried Line.

By turning east from Boisheim, we expected to reach the Rhine in the vicinity of Uerdingen, near the large industrial center of Krefeld (Map 11). From Boisheim to Uerdingen was another 20 miles. At Uerdingen, the Rhine made a horseshoe curve to the west, thereby bringing it closer to us. In order that we might use the most direct route, the northern half of Krefeld was included in the 84th's zone, though we intended to bypass Krefeld if possible in order to get to the river without delay. According to reconnaissance photos, the highway bridge at Uerdingen was still in operating condition. We had orders to seize it, cross it, and establish a bridgehead on the eastern bank of the Rhine.

Such was the position on March 1 as we looked back at the Roer and forward to the Rhine from the town of Boishem. Our men were tired, but men who were going forward as fast as we were could take a lot more tiredness than men who had to slug it out for a few yards a da

As far as Boisheim, the leading infantry unit in our advance was the 334th Infantry, although the other two regiments had plenty to do. They were following on foot, mopping up behind the tanks and trucks and jeeps. Whereas Task Force Church had driven a thin line through the enemy's territory on the main road, the follow-up forces had to negotiate a good deal of cross country, sometimes through thick woods. How thin that line was in some places was best illustrated by a sign prepared by some members of Task Force Church: "Road and Shoulders Only Cleared of Kraut." The fact that another regiment was able to take over the pursuit as soon as the 334th was given a slight rest was in itself an important achievement. It is necessary to go back in order to catch up with the 333rd Infantry which took over the advance from the 334th.

D-Day+6

Company E, the reserve element, was mopping up in 30 minutes. The forward companies, however, ran into heavier enemy artillery fire at the northern edge of Dülken. From high ground in the villages of Schirlck and Bistard, 88' s were blocking the way to Süchteln, the next objective. At this point, still another battalion joined in to push the pursuit. While the 333rd's 2nd Battalion moved around Süchteln on the western side, the 335th's 2nd Battalion went into Süchteln itself (Map 12). It should be emphasized that the 335th was moving on foot, without the assistance of tanks or reconnaissance troops for most of this operation, and yet it was able to move up with the motorized columns and to take our the chase on the shortest notice.

The 333rd's 2nd Battalion went out of Dülken first. Company F moved down the road to Bistard. A platoon of tanks from the 771st's Company B helped out. Whenever heavy small arms fire was encountered, the tanks would move ahead and wipe out the opposition. Whenever anti-tank guns were met, the infantry would leapfrog forward and knock them out, permitting the tanks to advance. Company C and another tank platoon took care of Schirick the same way. By the time both towns were cleared, it was dusk.

D-Day+7

At Süchteln, we were faced with another water crossing, a relatively minor one but enough to hold up our vehicles until bridges were put in. In our zone, the Niers Canal ran from south to north in three and sometimes in as many as five channels (Map 11). We planned to make a crossing at two places, one in the vicinity of Süchteln and the other in the vicinity of

Oedt, about 3 miles narth. At Oedt, we had to cross three channels, two on the west side of the town, one on the east side. This crossing was planned to protect our left flank as we pushed westward from Süchteln. At Süchteln,we had three channels to cross too but, once over, we could take advantage of the main road which led through Vorst, St. Tonis, and Krefeld to the

Rhine at Uerdingen.

All the bridges at both places were blown but there was one bridge in between that we were able to capture intact. The problems at both Süchteln and Oedt were similar. The first canal was 36 feet wide but the water was only 3 1/2 feet deep. The second canal was very small and could be forded easily. The third canal was approximately the same as the first one but it was guarded by anti-tank obstacles in the form of wooden railroad ties. Thus it was possible to cross infantry troops immediately, but to get the supporting armor across involved some delay. Engineers estimated that it would take 3 1/2 to 4 hours to build the bridges. In general, the crossings at Oedt were made by the 333m Infantry, those at Süchteln by the 335th Infantry. Both were fully over by March 2 or

D-Day+7

At Süchteln, the 335th's 2nd Battalion reached a bridge over the canal, about 800 yards east of the town, at about 3 am. on March 2. The infantry waded across and established a bridgehead about 600 yards deep so that the engineers could get to work on another bridge. By morning, the regiment was ready to push on again. Between Süchteln and Oedt, the 333rd's 2nd Battalion was sent out to capture the only bridge in the area that was still intact. The battalion left Bistard at 1 am. on March 2 and the bridge was taken, still intact, three hours later. The worst opposition came from the weather. It was snowing. Oedt itself was taken by the 333rd's 2nd Battalion late that afternoon. Organized enemy resistance was lacking but the occasion was notable for one reason. Oedt was the first town officially surrendered by the civilian officials. "When I entered the town," the battalion commander, Lt. Col. Norman D. Carnes, related, "the first man I met was a hotelkeeper. I asked him where the burgermeister lived. He pointed out the burgermeister's house farther down the street and said that he felt sure the burgermeister would see me. To that I replied, 'I know damn well he will. If you don't have him here in five minutes, both of you will be sorry.' Needless to say, the hotelkeeper brought the burgermeister on the double. The burgermeister had an interpreter with him but the interpreter was more interested in finding out whether or not I would permit him to open his velvet factory the next day than in translating for the burgermeister."

Once the Niers Canal was left behind, the entire division, led by the 335th Infantry, struck out for Krefeld, about 8 miles away. It was one of the easiest and quickest phases of the advance, resembling in many ways Task Force Church's breakthrough three days earlier. The change of direction from north to east seemed to catch the enemy by surprise again and few organized enemy units were encountered on the way.

But not for long. At about midnight, the infantry and tanks started out again, this time Company B's infantry in the lead and Company A's tanks in support. The column drove right into the northern sector of Krefeld without incident. Krefeld was quiet. The Nazis were not even able to defend an industrial center with a normal population of 160,000. In fact, the city fell so quickly that the municipal electric and water systems were still working. For the first time in Germany, 84th men saw running water. Dough-boys had to climb telephone poles to cut communication wires with the rest of Germany. Krefeld also produced the highest ranking prisoner to fall into our hands in 14 weeks. As Company C was advancing. a German staff car came down the road. The company commander, Lt. William B. Wood, ordered his men to open fire. The car stopped abruptly. Colonel von Bruske stepped out, his hands raised, shaking. The colonel explained that he was only a rear echelon officer but that he was ordered to the front to lead a battle group of the 176th Division. The 335th's 3rd Battalion followed the 1st Battalion into Krefeld and the 84th's half of the city was cleared by 5 am, March 3. The 102nd Infantry Division went into its half of Krefeld later that day but was not able to clear its area until the next day, March 4.

The next day, March 3, the 333rd's 1st Battalion, accompanied by the 771st's Company B, were ordered to take a roundabout route to Krefeld which enabled them to clear a few more important towns. From Oedt, this column went to Kempen, about 3 miles northeast. One of the strangest scenes in the campaign was witnessed in Kempen. As the column entered the town from the south, a few bursts of burp gun fire greeted the leading vehicles. The infantry and tanks immediately opened up. The column roared through the streets to the square in the heart of the town. In a church on that square, services were in progress. As the column passed by, everyone in the church came out, knelt on the steps of the church, and waved at our men with everything from white handkerchiefs to white sheets. This column continued eastward through Hiils, then turned south-east through

Bruckerhofe and Inrath into Krefeld. In effect, the whole

Krefeld area, for about 4 miles around, was paid a short visit. The general atmosphere was submissive and, on the part of many civilians, even cooperative. From Krefeld on, the army of white banners became a common sight.

Why Generals Get That Way

On March 2, when Krefeld became the next objective, the 84th was almost in sight of its original goal. The Rhine at Uerdingen was only about 3 miles from Krefeld. But that afternoon, a telephone call from higher headquarters forced us to make a lightning change in plan. It was the cause of the 84th's greatest disappointment in the entire battle of Germany. On March 2, the 84th was in a position to capture the first bridge across the Rhine. The Uerdingen bridge was still intact. In fact, the enemy was still using it. The staff had drawn up all the necessary plans and instructions for the plunge to the river and the establishment of a firm bridgehead on the other side. About 2500 yards east of the Rhine was a first-rate road. That was the objective. Even if the Uerdingen bridge was blown after the crossing, we were in a position to build another bridge because we held the high ground on the western bank. Lt. Col. Channon, 6-4, had arranged for planes to drop food and ammunition, if that proved necessary. The entire mission was approved by higher headquarters. A field order was issued. A special task force was organized, the emphasis on speed and power. It included an infantry regiment, the 334th, a whole tank battalion, the 77st. and a tank destroyer company. The 334th had been given a full day's rest at Boisheim.

This drive was set for 2 pm. All the men knew that they were starting off on an historic mission—the first bridgehead across the Rhine—and their hearts were set on it. General Bolling was there to wave them all. The sergeant in the lead tank handed him a thin cigar, saying: "Here, General, smoke this. Give me one across the Rhine." An MP detachment had cleared the road as far as Krefeld. The task force moved out. The tanks worked up to 25 miles an hour.

A few minutes later, the call came through. It was relayed to General Bolling by the chief of staff, Colonel Truman. Higher headquarters had decided to give the zone of the Uerdingen Bridge to the XIX Corps and to send the 84th to the zone farther north. The new order put us at the Rhine in the vicinity of Homberg. Instead of 3 more miles, we had about 11 more miles to go. Why this change was made is still obscure. General Bolling asked for reconsideration. The order was repeated. Homberg was not even on General Bolling's map at that moment.

It was too late to stop the Rhine-bound task force. One of the hardest and most dangerous maneuvers in the art of war was obligatory. It was necessary to reroute a huge column in motion. At the same time, it was necessary to make an immediate and equally far-reaching change in the work of the other two columns. Originally, the 335th had to take half of Krefeld, the

333rd had to protect the left flank of Krefeld, and the 334th had to drive through to the Uerdingen Bridge. Now, all three columns had to do something else. General Bolling had to call all three regimental commanders on a moment's notice, direct them to change their course, and give them altogether new missions about 10 miles away in a zone which they had never even considered. It was an intense, heartbreaking moment. General Bolling put through the calls. He gave the orders. The regimental commanders were barely able to believe their ears. The switch was made. The Uerdingen Bridge was swiftly forgotten. New maps were hunted up frantically. All eyes turned north, to Hornberg.

North Again

In our new sector, two bridges spanned the Rhine. The one farther north, the Baerl Railroad Bridge or Knippbrucke, was built for rail traffic and adapted for vehicle traffic. It was a five-span bridge and the Rhine at this point was approximately 1000 yards wide. The other, the Admiral Scheer Bridge, connected the cities of Duisburg and Homberg. It was a highwaybridge, 2050 feet long, 53 feet wide, with a road width of 38 feet and a water gap of 1600 feet. This type was known as a steel candelabra truss type bridge.

On March 2, while the 335th was moving on Krefeld, the 334th took charge of the new mission to Homberg. Its objective was the Admiral Scheer Bridge. In order to get there as quickly as possible, this column was ordered to bypass Krefeld and to strike out to the north from St. Tonia.

Once its job in Krefeld was finished, the 835th could move up from behind, pass through the rear of the 334th, and take a longer route on the left flank to the Baerl Railroad Bridge. The two bridges were about 3 miles apart. The 333rd was sent into Krefeld. It is interesting to note that the 334th had to fight its way out of St. Tonia, although the 335th had already passed through it. This was typical of the action from the Roer to the Rhine.

The leading elements would advance

along the main routes and reconnaissance elements would cover the flanks on the secondary routes. Nevertheless, pockets of enemy troops were often met by the units that followed up in the same general direction and no march was entirely uneventful. In this case, the 334th arrived in St. Tonis in the late afternoon, March 2. This column was spearheaded by the 334th's

1st Battalion, and the 771st's C Company. Northeast of St. Tonis, in the little village of Ortsmannsheide, the tanks ran into a pocket of enemy self-propelled guns and anti-tank weapons. A fierce fire fight held up the advance for four hours and the column had to reorganize in St. Tonis before it was safe to start out again. This time Company A's tanks took the lead. C Company's infantry walked ahead of the tanks, Company A's beside them, and B Company behind them.

"That night we had about the wildest night march you can imagine," said Captain B. C. Mills, commander of the 771st's Company C. Once more, an advance that was stalled in the daylight was not held up for more daylight but was started off again at night on a round-the-clock basis. The success of this maneuver was one of the outstanding features of the entire drive.

Again and again the enemy was powerless to stop us because he could not see us or because he was not prepared to do anything about it. By daylight, we were far out of reach, he was cut off, and apt to give up or to fight with much less enthusiasm against the second or third wave. By daylight, March 3, this column got as far as Klied, 5000 yards from the pocket at Ortsmannsheide. The most interesting stretch of this part of the trip was the road between the villages of Inrath and Klied. Apparently a German mine-laying detail was always one lap ahead of the advance. Five different hasty mine fields were encountered and it seemed that we were removing them a few minutes after they were laid. Fortunately, a large enemy ammunition dump was blazing away in the vicinity and its bright flames furnished some light.

At Klied, the 334th's 3rd Battalion, supported by the 771st's Company A, took the lead. For the daylight advance, one infantry company, L, rode the tanks, and the two others, I and K, the trucks. As usual, there was much more evidence of the enemy during the day than during the night. For this, however, there was now a special reason. The enemy was forced to recognize that the battle west of the Rhine was virtually lost. To save as much as could be saved was his last hope. To do so, he had to hold on to the Rhine bridges as long as possible in order to bring across to the relative security of the east bank the maximum amount of troops and equipment. By March 3, it was clear that the enemy was trying to form a line of resistance between Homberg and Uerdingen in order to protect the withdrawal across the Rhine. This mission was given to elements of the 15th Panzer Grenadier Division, the 406th Division, and miscellaneous paratroop units. As a result, some of the heaviest fighting in the drive suddenly flared-up in the very final phase of the operation.

At daylight, March 3, tanks and trucks moved out of Klied. It was still about 10 miles to the Admiral Scheer Bridge, more than half of them through a string of villages as far as Mors, the rest through the twin cities of M6rs and Homberg, in front of the bridge across the Rhine from Duisburg. This was the enemy's last crust of resistance west of the Rhine in our zone. The drive from Klied to the outskirts of Mors took the whole day. It was a running fight and the 834th's 3rd Battalion was forced to dismount at least twice to clear the way. The second and most serious battle occurred in the afternoon at a castle about 3 miles from Mors, Schloss Lajuersfort. There some German 88's, 20mm. anti-aircraft guns, and mortars stopped the advance of the tanks and brought the infantry into action on the ground. The 334th's 3rd and 2nd Battalions were both committed in the engagement. When it was over, the amount of German guns and equipment knocked out or captured showed that a real fight was waged. Two 75 mm. self-propelled guns and one 75 mm. towed gun, four 88's unmanned, three half—tracks, one flak wagon, one captured 2 1/2-ton U. S. truck with ammunition, and two 3 1/2-ton panel trucks were accounted for. Nevertheless, most of the enemy troops in the area were thoroughly confused and many prisoners were taken all day long. The column was held up at the chateau for a few hours but was able to get as far as one of Mors's suburbs, Mors-Vinn, by dusk. One tanker described the night of March 3-4 in the vicinity of Mors as "a wild night and a wild shooting party. Everyone was firing in all directions at once."

In any case, on the night of March 3-4, the cities of Mars and Homberg were practically all that stood between us and the Rhine in our zone. It was also clear that the enemy's efforts to build up a crust of resistance on the west bank of the Rhine were good but not good enough. The 84th's staff was able to breathe freely again. The last 24 hours had been gruesome. In order to obey the order to go to Homberg instead of the Uerdingen Bridge, one of the "forbidden" maneuvers in combat—"forbidden" in general staff' schools—was necessary. No fewer than three major columns had to be crossed at the same time. The 335th had to cross the 334th at the Bettenkamp road junction. The 333rd had to cross the 335th to get into Krefeld. The traffic problem was stupendous. Every member of the staff, including the chaplain, adjutant general, inspector general, and finance officer, was sent out to road junctions to keep the columns straight that night. The books said that it was impossible. Considering the circumstances, not only was it possible but it was achieved with amazingly little confusion.

The Rhine at Last

The last day of real combat in our zone west of the Rhine was March 4 or D-Day+9. That morning the enemy was holding only a 4-mile bridgehead, but the very momentum of our advance tended to throw us into sharp conflict against his relatively large forces that were jammed into the bridgehead, trying to escape over the bridges to the east bank. To follow the final drive, it will simplify matters to start with the unit that succeeded in reaching the Rhine first.

At daylight, March 4, the 335th's 2nd Battalion, which had sweated it out at the Bettenkamp road junction during the night, moved out toward Mors. It went through the southern part of the town without encountering more than scattered snipers who surrendered quite readily. A good deal of mortar fire, however, hit the town from the north. The first solid resistance was met at Meerbeck, a half mile east of Mors, about noon. From Meerbeck, the Baerl Railroad Bridge, its objective, was visible. A steady stream of traffic, mainly horse-drawn artillery, trucks, and many foot troops, was crossing over. Our artillery was called to put a stop to that. Time fire exploded into great flame-red flower-clusters of steel above the bridge, darting from the west bank to the east bank and back again. Several vehicles were knocked out and only foot troops tried to get across. But still the enemy did not blow the bridge.

Along the river were three railroad embankments. All of them were heavily defended and anti-tank guns covered all the possible approaches. At about 1 pm., Company B loaded on tanks and tried to charge up to the bridge but the anti-tank guns opened up and the tanks had to pull-back. About a dozen men of Company E, however, did reach the Rhine at 1:25 p.m., the first in the division to do so. Then one platoon of Company E tried to cross an open field between the first and second embankments but the enemy's fire was still too strong and this effort also failed.

It was necessary to wait until dark to pass Companies F and G through

Company E and move them all to the river bank. The battalion reached the Rhine with all three companies on line. Soon after, at 8 pm, the bridge was finally blown. It was still used by enemy foot troops until about 1 a.m., March 5, however, when a second explosion was heard. Company E came to the bridge area two hours later and confirmed that the bridge had crashed into the Rhine.

The 335th's 3rd Battalion came to the Rhine with somewhat more difficulty. At 9:30 p.m., March 4, it was ordered out of Meerbeck to seize a road junction at Lohmannsheide about a mile northwest of the bridge, which the enemy was using to withdraw from the north. As a result, although the Germans were bent on retreat across the river rather than resistance on the west bank, they held that area in much greater strength than elsewhere. At least 100 vehicles, including tanks, half-tracks, troop carriers, and trucks, moved through the road junction that night.

L Company was leading. About 800 yards from the objective. Captain Oreste V. Valsangiacomo stopped the company to check his maps. He went into a house along the road, fortunately through the back door, and found six German officers sitting around a table in the next room. It was an enemy CP. He left quietly, realized that the company had walked into the German lines, but decided to continue on to the road junction, hoping to slip through before the ruse was discovered. He was almost successful too. Soon, however, the Germans opened up with machine guns and small arms, the company was cut in two, and he managed to hit the road junction with 30 men. There, in the midst of the biggest enemy concentration in the entire area, they dug in for the night to wait for reinforcements. Company I and Company K came up later and also dug in near the road junction.

Since the bridge was blown that night and the 335th's 2nd Battalion was already holding a part of the river bank, the 3rd Battalion was sent to cleanout Baerl the next morning, March 5. It was empty. Captain Valsangiacomo found the rest of his company. Later in the day, the 8rd Battalion went into position along the Rhine.

As for the 334th Infantry, after the wild shooting party, the 3rd Battalion moved out on the morning of March 4 and headed for Homberg, arriving a about 7 pm. I Company received some fire from an enemy tank at an underpass at the edge of the town, but the tank pulled out and the company cleared out the right half of the town without resistance. K Company caught a platoon of German troops by surprise; some were running around Homberg without any weapons. I Company went into position along the Rhine at about 3 am. the next morning, March 5, K Company after daylight. The 334th's 2nd Battalion was held up south of Mors on March 4 by two 88's but managed to bypass them after dark and went on to the Rhine by about 5 a.m., March 5.

In the language of official reports, the 84th's drive from the Roer to the Rhine was told as follows:

"In ten days, February 23-March 4, 1945, the 84th Infantry Division advanced approximately 45 miles from Linnich on the Roer to Homberg on the Rhine."

"The 84th's breakthrough from Metzerath to Waldniel on February 27 was the first of its kind in the Battle of Germany."

"The 84th led the Ninth U. S. Army to the Rhine, its flanks almost always exposed because the flank divisions could not maintain the same pace."

"There were six distinct phases in the drive:
(1) February 23 — the Roer crossing
(2) February 25 & 26 — the first crust of resistance, Linnich to Matzerath
(3) February 27 — first breakthrough, Matzerath to Waldniel
(4) February 28-March 1 — second crust of resistance, Waldniel to Süchteln, Lt J. V. Morgia returned from the Paris Pass on March 1, 1945.
(5) March 2-4 — second breakthrough, Süchteln to Mors
(6) March 4-5 — last phase, Mors and Homberg"

"The total number of prisoners taken, February 23-March 5, was 5,445."

"Enemy equipment destroyed, captured or damaged for the operation included 40 FA guns, 21 88 mm. AA/AT guns, 21 75 mm. AT guns, 18 assault guns and tanks, 159 motor vehicles, 6 searchlights, 13 supply dumps, 7 destroyed and 2 probably destroyed enemy aircraft."

'The 84th Infantry Division was one of the very few divisions which fought the way from the Roer to the Rhine without losing its momentum for a single day."

The Roer River Crossing.

Platoon Crossing over the Roer.

CHAPTER 9
HOMBERG TO HANNOVER

The best thing that happened to the 84th infantry division was to sit on the Rhine River for about one month. Not only was it quiet, but was in a large city that was still in livable condition - placed on one side of the river that was wide and deep. The 84th troops were on the west side, which was free of German soldiers and also "safe" from soldiers on the other, east, side. This was the first real relief for the division in 15 weeks. The only duties that were assigned were guard duty and maybe going on a limited patrol.

Personal responsibility to themselves was number one priority; such as, maintaining their equipment and clothing. They even worried about getting a long needed haircut. They did not have to eat K or C rations because some of E Company kitchen staff rescued a local beer hall and served hot meals in the mess hall format. Of course, things got more interesting when steins of beer were added to the menu. I don't remember if they had sawdust on the floor. Definitely no spittoons.

E Company was lucky to have the best cooking leader, S/Sgt. James R Copley, from Coalgood, Kentucky. He was continuously in charge of the E Company kitchen during the whole war. He made the Army staples into gourmet dinners. I was assigned to be the mess officer in addition to my other duties, so I was able to get a closer look at his craft.

The volume of letters written to friends and family in the USA increased, but the officers still had to read and censor the information for security reasons. One of the Railsplitters reporters wrote, "Not more than 300 yards away from the enemy, doughs of the 84th, who slogged through mud of Brunssum and Geilenkürchen, who watched their feet swell in the frozen Ardenness, are now living and fighting from tiled bathrooms, deep cushioned easy chairs and six-inch boxspring beds covered with lace spreads." He forgot that a lot of mattresses and pillows were filled with feathers…

The entertainment extras included live popular performers, U.S.O. shows, Red Cross girls and donuts, along with local movie houses. I don't

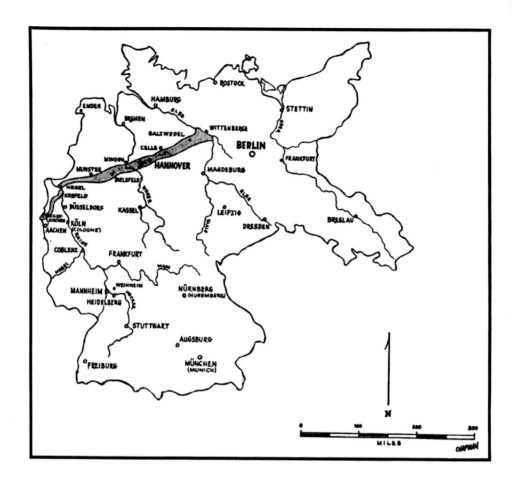

remember the popcorn. The first time in four months, the 84th was not directly involved in a major status during the battle of Germany. So the Rhine Crossing was anticlimactic compared to the Roer River crossing. The German forces were stretched out so the Allied concentration of force for the last phase of the European war was crushing.

On March 29, the 84th Division's role was to stay behind the 5th Armored. The armor can get through by avoiding heavy resistance and avoiding combing the whole area. Other divisions behind us had to clean out pockets of resistance. The fourth was given a dual role – to move up right behind the armor and to fight off the first signs of real resistance. East of the Rhine are three principal rivers; the Weser, Leine, and Elbe. The area is generally lowland of undulating planes with two ridges, or high ground system, passing through it.

The offense from the Rhine to the Weser, about 100 miles, was made in four days by most of the 84th division. After Weser River crossing, it experienced more clashes with the enemy. The main fighting took place at roadblocks that were hastily set up. The efficiency of the roadblocks depended on the covering fire for which, at best, was limited. They failed to hold up the advance of the combat troops. The average time for tearing down the block was 20 minutes, or more, for elaborate blocks.

The Task Force Church was motorized so that every unit moved like one part of a continuous train. However, there were many stop and go events. I remembered riding in the front seat of a Jeep. There was an endless number of stops. The stops varied in time length. I vaguely recollect where we were and what I did during that period, due to an increased lack of sleep. We were always in the vicinity of the vehicle. No enemy fire was encountered as we passed through the small towns along the way. Of course, everyone riding on jeeps or in 2 1/2 ton truck transports was armed and ready to respond to any trouble.

Currently the military government section under Maj. Frank Green, and our counterintelligence detachment, under Lieut. Charles Rountree, began to work overtime to set up responsible local leaders to maintain order.

The fight was not over in some areas, such as what was encountered on April 7 by the 334th 3rd Battalion in the 771st company A trucks, about 2 miles west of Bückeburg, they had to shoot their way through Roche. Other units had already passed through but the enemy had returned and set up a new position outside of town.

Company L was mounted on tanks and was forced to go house to house to clean up the dugouts. Lieut. Frederick M. McConnell, L Company's commander, said, "that for once in the drive from the Rhine to the Elbe, the enemy's resistance was fanatical". Some Germans managed to withdraw into the town, however, aided by artillery and tanks. The infantry took over the town of Roche. It was cleaned by noon and companies I and K moved through to get to Bückeburg.

A defensive line was established outside of town for the rest of the day and night. It was not often, in the drive from the Rhine to the Elbe, that the enemy's fire was so thick that our infantry could not stick their heads above the foxholes, but Bückeburg was one of those times. It is interesting to note that the experiences of the 335th and 333rd at Eisenberg on April 7 and the experiences of the 334th and 335th Bückeburg on April 8 were basically the same. When the first attack on the towns from one direction met strong and successful resistance, we encountered an attack from another direction.

The enemy gave in. The one-two punch was peculiarly effective. Apparently, the enemy was overwhelmed with the strong, swift follow-up which was too much for its morale. The town of Bückeburg was the anchor of its whole position and since it fell we were able to break out into the open again.

In the first 48 hours after the Weser crossing, April 6-7, the 84th traveled approximately 6 miles. In the next 24 hours, April 8, we covered approximately 25 miles. I still remember our column overtook an enemy convoy, halfway between Warber and Rusbend, which included several half-tracks, three trucks, and a tank. The half-track and tank were destroyed. Some of the trucks carried food. I ended up rolling out a 3 foot diameter cheese wheel. I put into my Jeep for future snacks.

"As we flushed Germans and motioned them to the rear, the men of Canon Company put the Nazis in the truck. When the truck became too full it was unloaded at the nearest MP post.

The First Battalion cleared Stadthagen by 0215, 8 April 1945. We had been moving continuously all night, and the armor leading the column was manned by quiet soldiers. As the Germans slept behind blackout shutters they heard the sound of our armor and did not hear any noises of battle. It was natural for them to believe the sounds they heard were their Panzer divisions moving about to meet the American offensive. The next morning the civilians opened their shutters amazedly to find American soldiers building fires along the road and cooking emergency rations. A few soldiers knocked on the door and asked for warm water for coffee and shaving. Wehrmacht rear echelon troops were awakened with varying gentleness from their beds, told to dress, and sent to PW cages at the rear of the convoy. Every house held a few soldiers, some of whom displayed discharges issued the day before.

The Regiment was approaching Hannover. Originally the Germans had intended to defend Hannover strongly. The outer defense was to be conducted in a circle of small villages which surrounded the town."

CHAPTER 10
TASK FORCE CHURCH POINT MAN

E Company, 334th infantry did very little walking as being part of the Task Force Church. The previous chapters describe the rapid advances in miles per day. On the eve of April 9, 1945, I found time to talk with Capt. Seymour B. Stone, Battalion Headquarters staff about the war in Europe winding down. He knew the big picture and he was happy about our future outlook.

"(That evening) Capt. Seymour B. Stone, Pfcs Edmund J. Brown and Douglas N. Jennings in a billeting team took on more than twice their strengths in Engelbostel. Capt. Stone, moved into Engelbostel directly behind the front lines to secure billets for the Battalion CP. As the Jeep containing Stone, his driver, Jennings, and his interpreter, Brown, moved down the street they noticed a house filled with Germans. Capt. Stone immediately dismounted, slung his carbine from the shoulder and pumped lead into the house which later we discovered held seven Nazis.

The Nazi's were preparing a machine gun nest to ambush the next troops moving down the streets. They were not quite prepared when the three men moved in on them. The Germans in the front yard ducked into the house and our men moved in on them.

The three Americans cleared the ground floor of the house. Jennings went to the cellar door and jerked it open. In the cellar below, traversing a machine gun to meet him, was a German soldier. Jennings reacted instantly. He drove down the stairs, kicked the machine gun to one side and fired a burst that killed the German.

During the encounter Capt. Stone was killed from a German automatic weapon's burst. All in all, the three men of Headquarters Second killed, captured, or wounded the seven Germans, and averted a possible ambush for the troops following behind."

At the same period of time, the division generals, General A. Bolling and General J. Church were planning the 334th Infantry advance into the northern part of the city of Hannover. The 334th Regiment played a heavy role along with assigned attachments. Every unit was directed to be ready to move at 0200 hrs. April 10, 1945 at the I.P. located at Engelbostel.

Usually the lead company for the column would designate a lead platoon to start the march. This time no vehicles were used by the infantry. Thus, every foot soldier walked. The mechanized units were kept behind the column to minimize the noise for the night's movement.

I was picked to lead the entire Task Force Church comprising of about 5000 men south on a very foggy night starting at 0200 hrs. There were no lights, no sound, no signs posted for this massive move. Our mission or objective was the largest city in this part of Germany, the city of Hannover.

I'm not sure how fast I was walking, but at one point of this advance, I noticed the German's autobahn road system ahead. Our road system passed underneath the autobahn. I saw a huge Tiger tank, Mark IV, on our road (under the Autobahn highway). Of course, my next move was to detour from our road and bypass the tank by walking over onto the autobahn and reentering the road on the other side of the tank. This simple maneuver was an instant reaction in a situation where many lives would be lost trying to overcome a Tiger tank. There was no inaudible way to discuss this unexpected enemy incursion for proper action.

The consequence of a wrong decision to overcome a Mark IV tank with protection overhead, would have invited them to turn their massive gun on our lined-up column of soldiers. It would have been very difficult and time-consuming to direct the counter fire necessary to destroy the Mark IV tank.

The episode ending in a very peaceful manner – after over half of the task force troops passed the autobahn – as the light of day appeared and some curious troops walked by the Mark IV tank and heard the sound of sleeping crew members. I was told that they all surrendered!

Further along on our approach into the city of Hannover I and my runner, Pfc. John McManus (Wooster, Mass.) moved cautiously into the city suburb. It was still dark but less foggy. I really did not know what time it was. A runner from Lieut. William W. Thompson approached me in a roadside ditch to report back to see Lieut. Thompson. I left, without my runner, to talk to Lieut. Thompson. Moments later, I heard the sound of a burp gun at the head of the column. My runner, Pfc. John McManus, and 2nd Lt. Harrel R. Needham were shot dead. Lt. Needham lead the foremost platoon in the task force.

These two close buddies were the only loss of this action into Hanover, Germany. The light of day became bright as we cautiously walked in a quiet city. There was no interference and there were a lot of white flags in some of the un-bombed building windows. Hannover was one of the most bombed-out cities in Germany. The devastation was widespread, but everyone cooperated.

I now understand why generals Church and Bolling trusted me to lead their powerful task force in the dead of the night to the largest German city, Hannover. They appreciated my actions at Beho and trusted my military instincts and leadership.

Hannover toward the end of the war.

CHAPTER 11
REPLACEMENT DEPOT
LIFE-SAVER ASSIGNMENT

My E Company left Hannover, that same day; April 10, 1945 for the Elbe River, which would be the ultimate destination as the war neared an end. After traveling several hours after departure, I received orders to return to Hannover and organize a replacement depot to lecture new troops, unfamiliar with combat.

The facility was in a German Kaserne "barracks" building. I remember talking to new troops and explaining how to cope and stay alive on the battlefield. There was no formal curriculum guidelines. Everything was in an impromptu manner. This assignment did not last very long, because by April 13 the war would be over and there would be no need for replacements or training.

My off-duty times were spent visiting the town's area close by with a regiment of 333rd American troops. I bought some art supplies in a nearby I.G. Farber factory. I also remember visiting the cellar of the German Kaserne and found thousands of detailed maps of Russia. Apparently, Hannover could have been the source of such printed matter. The cellar was used as an Army warehouse.

The warehouse contained other items of interest. The one which nearly gave me a Purple Heart was large amounts of mine detonators. I picked one up to check it out. Before had a chance to inspect it, it exploded and sent a few fragments to my face. Fortunately, it did not hit my eyes. I could have demanded the Purple Heart if it did. However, the flesh wound could be compared to a shaving razor knick.

In the meantime, the 84th Division experienced a lightning move on the last leg, going from Hannover to the Elbe River in three days. The attached map indicates a distance of 80 miles. Note that a total distance from the Rhine River to the Elbe River is approximately 250 miles. So, from April 1, 1945, the starting date on the Rhine, to the ending date on the Elbe, April 13, 1945, only about 13 days elapsed. The first segment's coverage per day, from the

Rhine to the Leine River, was 17 miles. From the Leine River to

Elbe River the average speed was 26 miles per day. Note that the Division operated three combat teams, the 333rd under Col. Lloyd H. Gomes, the 334th under Col. Charles E. Hoy, and the 335th under Col. Hugh C. Parker. However, the 335th, and myself, were left in Hannover as a XIII Army Corps reserve.

Besides the sporadic resistance from various German defense groups, thousands of inducted slave laborers from all over Europe were released from various locations. I think of it as Volks (People) Emancipation. I use the word "Volks" because it has a letter "V" in it. This "V. E. Day" preceded the official V. E. Day formally declared on August 8, 1945.

Author note: Russians reached the Elbe River on 2 May, 1945. The War was not won on the Elbe River. It was won at one point of the invasion of Germany between the Roer and Rhine Rivers.

The war, however, was not won on the Elbe River. It was won at one point of the invasion of Germany between the Roer and Rhine Rivers. That point was during a staff meeting held on the evening of D-Day plus three, February 26, to decide how to exploit the enemy's obvious disorganization to the utmost. Gen. Alexander Bolling had been playing with the idea for so long that only the remaining details needed to be finalized. The attitude among the Command had set our objectives in terms of miles not yards. We were thinking in terms of task forces; a miniature Division. Each infantry regimental unit had its own tanks, artillery, engineers, and air observers. The result was Task Force Church. It was commanded by the assistant Division commander, Gen. John church. It was the first fully motorized task force of the Division.

In hindsight, the payoff of the breakthrough on February 27 spared many American and German lives. Not only did it save lives but the war in Europe was shortened, in my estimation, by at least one month. I must take some credit for this based on my contribution leading my troops instrumental in stopping the Germans in its intent to wipe-out the 84th Division troops housed in the town of Beho, Belgium on the night of January 22-23, 1945. I like to think that I kept the Railsplitter's axe blade "sharp" to allow "cutting" through the enemy defenses.

Gen. A. Bolling by the Elbe River, Germany.

CHAPTER 12
PX OFFICER POSITION

On VE Day, the Army Exchange System was operating in the European theater under the oversight of G-I Division, US Forces, with headquarters in Paris, France. The priority was to provide exchange services for thousands of troops in Europe. The AES in Germany would have to replace civilian facilities. The Post exchange officers must be appointed by the local Division commanders and were responsible to them. In the V-E Day period the approved plan was to transfer the community exchanges from direct control of the Army Exchange Service to that of the local community commander until a new plan was developed.

The headquarters eventually moved from Paris to relocate in the heart of the US troop concentration in Hoechst, Germany, in the suburbs of Frankfurt. The running of an overseas exchange in those days existed within a sea of rubble and shorthand economies. Currency was worthless. Stores were empty. Where goods were stored pilfering was rampant. The black market was everywhere and most items were strictly rationed. Many people use cigarettes for services, laundry, etc. while patronizing the black market. Some of the items were rationed to the G.I.'s because they were very valuable sought after goods.

I did not have an opportunity to join my E Company, 334th unit during their stay on the river near the town of Balow during the VE Day celebration. I was transferred from duties as replacement Depot instructor to a position of PX officer for the 334th infantry Regiment. Eventually they were repositioned to the Heidelberg Rhine area of Germany in occupation troops status (Uberbach on the Neckar River). The men were billeted in nearby homes with the company kitchen unit nearby. The officers located themselves in a comfortable home with many rooms overlooking the river. I was billeted in a small apartment in the Karlsvuhe area. I was instructed to ration a trailer truck load of PX items to various units within the 334th infantry Regiment. The items included many goods such as candy, cigarettes of many brands, watches, cameras, personal items, etc. Every individual soldier was sure to get an equal ration of cigarettes and candy however special items such as watches or cameras were limited in number. For example, a Company could end-up being supplied only two watches.

The units were called to send a vehicle to my location with money to pay for the PX goods. Naturally, no one hesitated to buy their share of the goodies. The process took several days of my time and I waited for the next trailer load for distribution. This method of PX distribution was a temporary set up until a better system came along. The problem with the system was that the commander had to trust the person in charge. I heard stories that a soldier going on pass to a city like Berlin would be offered many German marks for a wristwatch or pack of cigarettes.

Not only did Gen. Bolling get a trusted shopkeeper and taking me out of harm's way, but I was a good organizer to supply the troops what they craved. I still remember as a young teenager, about 13 years old, helping my mother take care of a small grocery store.

I would make sure all the stock was arranged properly and help with making sandwiches for some local workers. I would machine slice the boiled ham, cheese, and tomatoes and place them into a crispy six-inch "knobby" bun, all for 25 cents. Nowadays people call them "grinders".

I don't know how long I maintained the PX position, but after I was relieved I returned to my old E company with Lieut. William W Thompson in Eberbach on the Neckar River, located about 20 miles east of Heidelberg, Germany. I rejoined my fellow officers in E Company in a resort (sort of) town nestled in the river valley. When I got there I received a couple of boxes of pepperoni one which my mother sent me. It must've been in route to me over several months and I was the only one to enjoy it, at first. Later everyone was asking for it. Too late, it was all eaten!

Besides the "Mama-Mia" grinders, that little store had a back room with a few tables where friends would come in for a plate of spaghetti and meatballs with sauce cooked by my mother. My father "cooked up" a barrel (55 gallons) of wine each year so that it went with the meal. We even had a private "pull line" from the store to our cold railroad room apartment on the fourth floor with the bell at the end to signal for help in the store. "Ma-bell" was three pulls on the wire.

The preceding events happened when I was 13 years old. The year before, when I was 12 years old, I spent the entire summer as an adult worker raking 89 golf course sand traps each day. At that time in 1934, we had no store. I lived in the maintenance garage with an elderly family friend who mowed and took care of the greens. We did our own cooking. At times, I made cucumber or banana sandwiches for lunch.

During the work off hours, I would caddy for the Fenway Country Club members to make more money. I remember one encounter with the course foreman when he asked me how many traps I did that day. I replied, "I did 88 traps." He would remind me that "there are 89 traps on the course". "I know", I would say, "but I didn't want to get bee-hind." Note: There was always at least one sandtrap that became a nest for bees and hornets.

I still remember one day when I was 6-years old and home alone and hungry. There were only some potatoes and eggs in the kitchen, so I grated them and mixed it with an egg and fried up some potato pancakes on our gas stove. Many times I would make popcorn on our stove and melt butter on it. I still remember my father cooking spaghetti in a big pot of water and sampling some strands to check its "done-ness". When it was finished, all the strands were gone.

CHAPTER 13
ODD EVENTS WITHOUT DENTS

Not only did I face and cheat death and injury during the war, I also faced it several times before and after the war during my lifetime. In my young civilian life I can say that the occurrences that came upon me were due to my inexperience especially when the mind is focused on distractions which minimizes attentiveness. This is exactly what caused the near end to my life more times than I would like to think about but not as many as a cat was born with. I remember when I was old enough to buy a used two-wheeled bicycle and keep it repaired. Our family never owned an automobile so we either walked, biked, or rode the bus from town to town. One summer day, I took a leisurely ride on my bike on a sharp turn downhill road which converged with the main road along the side of the river. I was more focused on the river as I coasted down the hill. At the same time, an automobile was touring and keeping on the right side and did not see me because of the road's elevation. I did not see the automobile and the driver didn't see me until the last moment when the car hit my bike head-on with the right fender. At the last moment, I jumped from my bike onto his right fender and slid down the car's running board, unharmed. The driver was sympathetic and I said "you're not to blame". He left apologetic and I junked my bike, which was crushed. Back to walking.

When I graduated from Warren Harding High School, Bridgeport, Connecticut in 1940, I sought jobs that paid well for the summer to earn my tuition fees for The University of Connecticut. In 1941, when I was 19 years old, I found a job as a carpenter's helper with the Hardy Construction company, in Stratford, Connecticut. Instead of hammering nails, I spent most of my time digging water pipe and drainage trenches to the house and other heavy-duty work like pouring freshly mixed concrete, with a deep wheelbarrow, on a gang plank runway to make a foundation for the building. One day while carrying two heavy one-third square of roof shingles to the top roof section of the two-story building, I started to slip off the roof and one of the Hardy boys yelled "spread wing". I spread out on the roof to maximize the surface area and, hence, increase my friction with the roof. It averted me from sliding down off the roof to the ground below which was a drop of twenty feet. I don't know if this is fate, but after the war and NYU, I took a job at Sikorsky Aircraft Company where I met the secretary and typist in my office named Alice Hardy. She was the wife of the same Hardy boy who saved my life. He had passed away leaving her alone to care for her kids and aging parents. I felt compelled to pay them back by being "Alice's Alarm Clock"; calling her every morning and driving her to work. She was overworked by holding a full-time job and taking care of her aging parents and two grandchildren. It was the least I could do for her!

The next year, 1942, when I was 19 years old, I found another demanding job. It was a no-brainer job but it required a lot of muscle and stamina. It was at an asphalt mixing plant in Bridgeport, Connecticut. Ordinarily, this plant which processed clean sand by heating it in a large revolving kiln and mixing it with a hot liquid petroleum product to make hot asphalt. This was dropped into a dump truck positioned below the mixing chamber. The extraordinary circumstance with this job was that the company, Godfrey Asphalt Plant, was contracted to pave the town of Stratford's airport runway. It was an all summer job where 150 tons of mixed hot asphalt material was required each day. Now, me and a young son of the foreman, named John DeSouza, had to shovel this vast amount of sand into a continuous chain of buckets from an overhead sand storage bin. This was one hot summer with plenty of overtime. From time to time, the sand would not flow with the hand-operated bin gate open so someone had to get into the vent and move some sand. One day, I happened to slide with the moving sand while in the sand bin. Mr. DeSouza happened to be at the building's window above and yelled to his son to shut the bin gate. I was saved from an untimely fate by suffocation under the sand.

I did not know it at the time but I was essentially in training for the war that was brewing in Europe. This is post-Pearl Harbor where in Bridgeport the Chance-Voight company was building Corsair fighter aircraft and an airport was urgently needed. My brother, Nicholas, two years younger than me, worked in the Remington Arms factory making ammunition. This company was around the block and walking distance from our home. I was supporting the war effort already! Furthermore, Bridgeport was one of the four cities on the US East coast to be bombed by the enemy.

You can probably go through war without getting a scratch and return to civilian pursuits fraught with danger. I had my share of close calls involved in my civilian life.

While studying for my Master's degree at New York University in 1948, I decided to take a job with the Edcan laboratories in Norwalk Connecticut. I was now 26 years old and still did not have a driver's license. I had to take a train to commute to my workplace and classes in New York City. Every chemical product that we chemists produced at Edcan laboratory for delivery to our customers was made in batches. There was no assembly line, just a worktable for each chemist to mix and react chemicals that resulted in an end product. Some batches may create fumes that must be made in a special exhaust hood with wired safety glass sliding doors. I cannot forget being by the side of my fellow chemist, Dr. Charles Stern. I left the room for a smoke on the front steps and there was a loud explosion. Charles' twenty-two liter batch of chemicals exploded, spewing chemicals and glass about the laboratory. Later, I visited him in a New York hospital and he had vision problems which resulted from the blast. I cannot help but think what would have happened to me if I had not gone out for a smoke. This could probably be the only incident ever known where smoking a cigarette actually prolong one's life!

After I graduated from New York University with my Master of Science degree I started to work at Sikorsky Aircraft Company in Bridgeport, Connecticut where it started production to build military helicopters. The many materials used to build the helicopters required special chemical treatment before being primed and painted. My job was to analyze the concentration of chemicals in the reaction tanks once per week. Samples were taken for each reaction tank to the metallurgical laboratory for me to analyze. A given volume of sample liquid was pipetted into a test tube to determine the concentration. This particular liquid had poisonous cyanide in it. The problem occurred while mouth-pipetting the sample, the tip of the pipette came out of the solution, making the cyanide solution volatile in the column. I did not know if any of that liquid reached my mouth. I went to the plant's nurse. After asking me to sit down for a few minutes. After ten minutes the nurse looked at me and said, "You'll be fine." If I had ingested any cyanide I would have been dead within that time.

I was also very busy outside of my engineering job to personally manage and maintain nine family housing units in two buildings which my parents had left to me. The activity continuously occupied my spare time to cope with the ongoing problems with the tenants. Most of the tenants who were barely paying the rent were not very resourceful. It was a no-win situation and no one was interested in buying the properties. This "second job" lasted for over twenty years. I was plumber, electrician, carpenter, and overall property manager. I personally installed gas pipes, replaced water heaters, replaced roof shingles, and installed aluminum storm windows as high as three stories on an aluminum extension letter with screws in my mouth and one hand on the ladder. My family always worried about my time spent on these units where drug users and crime flourished. Some would even approach me if when I was outside, but I always had my carpenter hammer stowed in my pants belt. My combat experience served me well. Actually, this was worse than combat, since there were no 'front lines'.

I had always given the tenants the benefit of my good nature and support. One of the few times I had to evict a tenant was when this nice person, Norman, said he could not pay his rent that month because someone had robbed his delivery truck causing the owner to deduct it from his pay. Later on he lost his job and could not pay his rent so I had to evict him. During the eviction, his son broke into the sheriff's car parked in front of the apartment house and stole the sheriff's cash which was laying on the front seat. Upon cleaning-out the apartment, I found over 200 empty crack cocaine vials in the apartment cabinet. This was more disturbing to me in that he misrepresented himself to me as an honest person. But, giving it more thought, I realized that he was the victim of his own weakness.

I felt a duty to stay with the apartments because my father bought these houses with the money he had saved working as a steam-operated electromagnetic crane to pick up scrap metal from a river barge and load gondolas for trips to melting furnaces at the Stanley Works plants. Many times the replacement worker would not show up and the foreman Mr. Scheyd was happy that my father would do double duty. I still remember walking over to him a plate of spaghetti and meatballs at times when he was doing triple duty (a period of 24 hours).

My father's demanding job wages were compounded in the bank. He was a diligent saver who never owned a car, never went on vacation, never ate at restaurants, or paid for college. The properties where we lived contained all the things reminiscent of being back in Italy; an extensive vegetable garden, grape vines, fig trees, and wine making facility in the basement. With my help, he filed a tax return every year.

This was my education for my do-it-yourself nature. No one was available in my family or group of friends to advise me or plan my future. I never read fiction, I only subscribed to Popular Science or Popular Mechanics magazines. I never really played cards or games. I really had no extra time available for leisure activities. On Sunday's, when at that time all the stores were closed by law, we relaxed at home and enjoyed a good meal with family.

Umberto Morgia operating electromagnetic crane, 1946.

Umberto standing on a magnet, Stanley Works Yard, 1946.

CHAPTER 14
ALWAYS REACHING FOR THE BRASS RING
ABOVE & BEYOND

I became a responsible person early in life. When my parents were working their jobs, I would keep the house clean and take care of the garbage. I scrubbed floors at times on my hands and knees. I even helped my father paint the kitchen and bathroom. The landlord only offered free paint; green and dark brown. My father painted the kitchen green all over and I painted the bathroom cubicle dark brown. Most of the time I volunteered to help. Sometimes it was a direct order.

It was something about those times that helped instill in me a sense of self-motivation - a basic characteristic that made a big difference in my life. It help keep me going through the battlefield and the unexpected, and has kept me routinely active all the way to my current age.

In the pre-teen years, when weather got real cold, I would get newspaper and stuff the windows to preserve the little heat avail- able in our four room railroad, slum apartment. On my own, I would collect kindling wood during the year to save for starting kitchen stove fires with authentic coal. Of course, I had to take care of the ashes from the fire. When cold got colder we would put blanket covered chairs around the stove and make popcorn. The only good thing about the four-story, Victorian-era home was that it faced south. The ridge in front of the window was great for drying tomatoes. The last unheated room was an excellent place to make and store homemade root beer.

At about 5 or 6 years old, I walked to a local grade school, about five blocks away, myself. I associated with all students at school and on the playground. I never had them over to my house. I never recited in class because the teacher would always call on students beginning with the letter "A" or starting with the letter "Z". Since "J" and "M" were in the middle of the alphabet I was never called. I used to sell papers for the Bridgeport Post and the Times Star and shine shoes with my homemade shine box and stand. At times, when I had my shoe shine stand, I would count the number of freight cars on the train going by. I never got to count them all, because a shine customer would need my attention sooner than the caboose. A tavern located nearby would keep me busy and fed me with free pretzels. I applied this technique with the Salvation Army, receiving free donuts and coffee.

At the end of grade school, everyone had to decide their curriculum in high school. It was either business, college preparatory, or com- mercial courses. I chose the college curriculum in Warren Harding high school in Bridgeport without consulting with my parents first. Very few students had intentions of going to college. I had to take science, chemistry, languages (Latin and German) and advanced mathematics courses, which all affected my life for many years to come. Many friends that I associated with chose the business or commercial courses.

I enrolled at the University of Connecticut, which was known at that time as Connecticut Agricultural College, the previous year by visiting to sign up and take an IQ test in a single visit. I was accepted to start in September 1940 in the freshman class. I was housed in the Old Shakes House located off campus on a hill near a huge water tower. I had to walk back and forth at least twice daily. At times I would meet a friend, Sherman Chase, who liked to play ping-pong at the community house, located about halfway.

We were both great ping-pong players and had the whole place to ourselves without interruption. The following two years' extra-curricular activity was learning to play soccer. I found myself running around the soccer field for about two hours per day. I like soccer over the other sports because I consider myself to be undersized for sports such as basketball or football. The sport made me a better competitor. It undoubtedly shaped me for my years in the Army. When it came time, I ran through the Fort Benning obstacle course back in 1944 in great time. I never clocked myself, but I was faster than my classmates.

There was a requirement for graduating UConn in four years, which was taking the preliminary ROTC courses in the first two years. Every male took the Reserve Officer Training Corps' basic army training. To qualify to become reserved commissioned officers you had to enlist to take the third and fourth year courses. Upon graduation one could become a second lieutenant commissioned officer in the Army. There were 1944 class was interrupted by the Pearl Harbor attack and other deteriorating events around the world. My group of ROTC students finished their third year of college courses and were shipped to Camp Wheeler, Georgia in 1943 for basic training for 17 weeks. After that, we are sent to the officer's candidate army school in Fort Benning Georgia for another 17 weeks of training to be commissioned as second Lieut.

After the war in Europe and prior to my Honorable Discharge, I was given an opportunity to join the reserves with promotion to the rank of Captain. I told the recruitment officer that I would accept only if I could change my military occupational specialty to the chemical corps. He agreed and accepted. A few years later I received a letter saying that I would be transferred to the artillery MOS. I reasoned in my mind that I could be back in the infantry because of my experience, although it was after the war. So I sent in my resignation with the reserves. Sometime later, the Korean War broke out.

A current acting general, Brigadier General John Church was an experienced artillery soldier. At that time, he may have had a hand in pulling me over to the artillery corps. Were it not for this inter- ruption in service I may have been reenlisted into another war.

My years in the metallurgical laboratory at Sikorsky aircraft company were challenging because in a new industry that was growing many shop workers had problems that needed answers. It was not enough to put a Band-Aid answer to the problem because it was necessary to satisfy the customers' specifications. The customer was the United States Army. We had a simple communication procedure which was an AVO – avoid verbal orders. This simple form of communication does it all without misunderstanding problems and solutions.

In the beginning, experienced workers knew the procedure but as the workforce expanded it was necessary to write detailed procedures known as Sikorsky manufacturing standards. I found myself writing many standards which met military specifications. At times, when problems were resolved, I would improve the process for a variety of reasons. I took responsibility for such actions.

I designed and built processing tools, equipment, and processing tank systems during my 32 years. Unofficially, I was the chief chemical process engineer at Sikorsky Aircraft Company. Those days it was unethical to tattletale on others. I did what is common practice today. When I saw something I would say something. There was a time I remember when a Blackhawk helicopter crashed and no one knew why. I made a single two minute telephone call to an engineer staff member and the problem was solved. That happened over 30 years ago, after which Sikorsky had built 3,000 Blackhawks without failures. No one knows, besides this one man, but I became the unknown and silent Blackhawk godfather whilst the member I had contacted came to be a large player in the company.

I started my family life at a later date. My wife, Mae, was also a family helper. She is a beautiful, dedicated homebuilder. She walked all of my five darling children; Jeanine, Rina, Albert, Joan, and James to the local grade school four times each school day. On visitor's night, the teachers used to say to me, "I hope that some other parents would visit our school like you do." Mae never drove a car.

Besides serving as president of the church's Holy Name Society once a month for several years, I was active in the Holy Rosary Church singing

Morgia at America's Got Talent at 88, NYC, 2011

James in 1946.

UConn ROTC at Camp Wheeler, GA.

choir. Choir consisted of a mixed group of adults that usually sang religious songs during the high masses and spe- cial holidays. The offshoot of my singing episode was a desire to perform on the national television shows for prize money. I was among the many contestants of the X-Factor and America's Got Talent audition several years ago without success. The closest I got was through a third round of auditions singing Frank Sinatra's "My Way". Both my parents loved to sing. My dad used to play his mandolin and sing old Italian songs at home after his meal. When I was a very young child he told me to sing with him and I said that I don't know how. He replied in Italian not to worry…just do it. The rest is history as they say!

For the talent shows, I'm sure that I could never be the winner because there is a lot of talent out there. The key thought has to be that at 91 years of age I could still be able to compete. I've not tried to compete for several years since I stay close to home to attend family matters. However, I have on several occasions and local public assemblies sang the national anthem with great reception. I loved being with the people.

For me the key to aging gracefully is to keep moving, keep dreaming of new things to do, new challenges. Set your sights on ideas and projects and put together the tools that you need to accomplish those goals. Let us not forget that good health is the foundation of a life well-lived. Good nutrition and good habits started early. Set yourself up for a healthy second and third act of your life. If your time is not spent at doctor's appointments, then you are left to pursue other goals and aspirations.

Besides playing soccer at UConn, I kept active in indoor sports.

Here's a list of some of my athletic awards:

1972, bowling | Sikorsky mixed league - FIRST PLACE

1988, bowling | Railsplitter Convention - HIGH THREE GAME SERIES (handicap)

1993, ping pong | Holy Rosary Church Men's Club - RUNNER -UP

1994, bowling | Railsplitter Convention (Salt Lake City) - MENS HIGH GAME

Wedding Day: Mr. & Mrs. James V. Morgia, May 8 1952.

CHAPTER 15
THREE DAY TANK-LESS BOEING SOLUTION

For thirty-two years I was employed at Sikorsky Aircraft Company. Every day brought different challenges and I was never bored. Besides being the unofficial chief chemical engineer, I was also known as the "tank commander". Sikorsky had a chief engineer to design helicopters. But the surface treatment and finish of materials also held great importance and gave integrity to the aircraft. At that time, formally trained chemists in the manufacturing environment were not so common among the engineering community.

The tank commander oversaw the functioning of over 160 individual tanks within the two Sikorsky plants in Stratford and Bridgeport of varying sizes. Some tanks were as long as 40 feet to accommodate 36-foot long helicopter blades. The tank solutions varied with acids, alkalis, rinses, and metal plating in addition to temperature controls and exhausts. Therefore, the proper tank design and fabrication were important for successful and trouble-free operation. I was able to save millions of gallons of potable water each year by simply outfitting many reaction tanks with mist rinse nozzles so as to not pollute the rinse tank water.

The greatest challenge that earned me the title "walking on water" by my fellow chemist, Mr. Hugh Morris, happened when the Pratt & Whitney jet engine company could not deliver finished engines to outfit Boeing aircraft in Seattle, Washington. Dozens of ready-to-fly model "7XX" series aircraft were parked on the Boeing flight field with heavy concrete weights to prevent flipping. Awaiting a final solution to outfit the finished engines - they were grounded indefinitely. The Boeing Company was fining Pratt & Whitney millions of dollars each day for these delays. So, the old saying in business "time is money" fit this situation nicely.

The problem was that if we followed normal procedure and lead times, we were looking at several months to design, procure, and take delivery of the special tanks required for the process.

The engine parts were large seven foot diameter stainless steel rings with noise suppression material bonded internally. In order to properly bond, it was necessary to etch the ring using hot sulfuric acid followed by a water rinse and immersion into nitric- hydroflu- oric acid followed by a rinse. After drying, the parts were ready for the bonding process. The 7 foot diameter test piece was sent to the Bridgeport plant for processing in a 9 foot deep tank but the Pratt & Whitney engineers wanted the part that was one foot high to be immersed flat. Our existing tanks were not that wide. We did not have an 8 foot square tank. It would take at least a month for vendor to fabricate such a tank. Some of the tank lining material sheets required must be made of polypropylene and polyvinyl, which was difficult to procure in the state of Connecticut. These polymers have only recently been made

Morgia inspecting Sikorsky Aircraft machine shop.

available in large sheet forms. I must add that I had in-depth knowledge and fascination of polymer chemistry.

The proper choice of material for processing tanks helped to keep the tanks operational for a longer period time. I used to advise the maintenance department on the proper choice of materials for fabrication equipment.

Fortunately, I had in the Sikorsky plant enough 4 foot by 8 foot polypropylene and same size polyvinyl sheets to make two acid reaction tanks at 8 foot by 8 foot by 2 foot. I ordered a stainless heating coil for one tank which was readily available. Our tool room personnel did a fantastic job to weld the sheets and support the bottom and sides with steel cables and 2 inch by 4 inch wood - delivering them to the Bridgeport facility in two days.

The tanks were positioned in a basin area with an overhead crane next to a plastic swimming pool I had procured; to use as a spray rinse tank. It was highly unorthodox to bring in a kids swimming pool but it worked! I mixed the hot etching sulfuric acid solution and the desmut hydrofluoric-nitric acid solution and the seven-foot diameter jet engine rings were processed per specification for bonding and test at Pratt & Whitney aircraft company in Hart- ford, Connecticut. The results of this process and the subsequent bonding of the sound suppression material completed the requirements for use on the Boeing Aircraft.

The Pratt and Whitney JT9D engine "opened a new era" in commercial aviation. The high-bypass-ratio engine went on to power wide-bodied aircraft. I am proud that I could be able to conquer this unusual, unexpected problem in improving the famous P&W engine in record breaking time. It really is very easy for a design engineer to put it on paper-print, but someone, as they say…"has to make it happen". Again, I was that DIY guy.

Again, I will only take credit for one simple thing with this story about the great P&W JT9D engine, I saved Sikorsky 'three days of time and money' with their best customer, Boeing.

Mission accomplished in three days!

Launch of Titan IIIC, 1965.

CHAPTER 16

FROM THREE DAY LAYOFF
TO BOOSTER PRODUCTION

A s it is known throughout the industry, the helicopter business had its *ups and downs*.

In 1961, helicopter production dropped at Sikorsky Aircraft and consequently a reduction in workforce occurred. Since some departments were affected more than others, my job was elimi- nated from the design engineering department. For three days I sought employment elsewhere inside and outside the company. I was contacted by Mr. John Harvey, the group leader in the man- ufacturing engineer department at Sikorsky. He requested me to join his group to help build the Titan IIIC booster portion of the Saturn rocket. John was a wonderful man, colleague, and friend of mine for many years. Martin Marietta was the prime contractor on this major project for the government. Sikorsky needed this sub- contract in order to keep the reduced workforce employed. This project, of course, was not something we had experience with but the basic elements of material processing still applied; just more creatively then what we were used to.

Since our design engineering department in those days was not typically directly involved in the manufacturing process, I was tasked with conceiving the booster material finishing requirements with our manufacturing equipment capability in mind and exe- cuting to a finished product. Design for Manufacture was not yet

a known concept in engineering. The booster required a critical element, the heat shield, to allow it to operate at the extreme high temperatures. The heat shield needed to function properly and flawlessly to protect expensive equipment on the booster. Without it, the rocket would not function as intended. Eventually, all the elements in the project meshed to produce the Titan IIIC booster at the Sikorsky production facilities in Stratford and Bridgeport,

Connecticut. However, there was one very difficult requirement to comply with; the application of a special silicone material of vary- ing thickness between 20 and 200 thousandths of an inch. This was an application nightmare and to my knowledge was never done prior in the industry. The areas that required different thicknesses were close to each other and the only known means at the time of applying this ablative mix was by spraying using paint equipment due to the irregular surface contour. The thick build-up would be impossible to achieve and the overspray would be a big waste of material which cost in excess of $120/gallon. This special silicone material was manufactured by the Dow Corning company near Fort Knox, Kentucky. Not only did it have heat resistant silicones in it but also had micro-ceramic ball fillers. Their chemist showed me the spray equipment to apply the material but I knew it would not work for our application.

Since Martin Marietta designers specified thicknesses on a 4-foot by 6-foot convoluted ribbed and curved aluminum sheet, this would be extremely difficult for a hand-held paint sprayer to meet the finish thickness requirements. The Martin Marietta and Dow engineers helped as best they could but could not devise the equipment to meet requirements. I was alone to figure out how to meet this requirement. Instead of battling with the spray process, I decided to change the process. I devised a special tool to apply the silicone ablative compound to the specified thickness with good adhesion on the fabricated heat shield. The tool consisted of a reinforced fiberglass epoxy mold which took its shape from a sample part layered with built-up wax sheeting which represented the drawing specification.

The new mold tool was clamped to the heat shield and the catalyst mixed silicone material was pumped into the varying gap between the heat shield to be coated and the special tooling. When the ablative coating cured, the mold was removed and the finished shield was ready for use or shipment. There were many other problems which had to be solved in order to finish the metal parts of the heat shield. Most of these parts were made of aluminum which where heat treated for strength and it required special chemical bath treatments to promote paint primer adhesion. The chemical baths were modified so that the primer and top coat would pass the wet tape tests. The wet tape adhesion test consisted of the following: After the paint had dried for 24 hours, a water soaked cloth under a watch glass was placed on a painted surface for a period of 24 hours. A special tape placed on the test area would be used to try and remove the paint. If no paint loss was found, the test was deemed successful. The Titan IIIC Booster would power the world's first successful aerospace craft to reach the moon!

Another huge problem that occurred was the phosphate treatment of a 10 foot diameter ring which was very heavy and difficult to manipulate in a treatment tank. Sikorsky Aircraft manufacturing facilities did not have the space or the tanks to treat such a large object. This was another impossible task to meet the drawing spec- ification. However, I developed a spray procedure to accomplish the same results as the dip process. Management was grateful that Sikorsky Aircraft was able to do the whole job using existing equip- ment within the plant. I am very proud that I was able to do all the necessary work that successfully took men to the moon. Furthermore, most of these booster parts fell back to earth into the ocean and recovered to be used over and over again. This attests to the durability of the parts.

My resourcefulness and personal attention and commitment allowed this project to be successful. Knowing what was available, the options, and the risks, created a positive outcome; not much different than what I experienced twenty years before. But at the time, I really didn't make this connection. I knew the "objective" but the game plan was all on me. Maybe the spirit of General Church was watching over me.

CHAPTER 17
BELGIUM 2.0 AND 3.0: RETOURS

Return to Europe #1: Aug 01-Aug 22, 1990

This is a great time for me to add that I have been in Europe with my son Jim. Jim had just graduated from Rensselaer Polytechnic with a Master's degree in Engineering and I thought it was a good idea for him and me to take a European summer vacation. We decided to spend 21 days to visit seven countries. Our Lufthansa plane landed in Frankfurt, Germany on the same day that Kuwait was invaded by Sadam Hussein's Iraqi forces. The airport was surrounded with armed guards but we stayed on plan to rent an automobile; a 1990 Mercedes-Benz 190E. We had no reservations and no plans, but decided to visit the old Siegfried line in the Geilenkirken area of Germany. I had a large video camera with me and for some unknown reason the camera would not take pictures. It made me think about the dead people. I later found out that I forgot to put the on button to start the motion picture mode.

The seven countries visited were The Netherlands, Germany, Switzerland, France, Italy, Austria and the important focal country of Belgium. We drove over 3,000 miles. I made sure that we visited the Heidelberg and Eberbach areas where we spent much time as occupation troops before returning home to the United States. We next went south to Switzerland and spent about three days in their capital city and Basel. Next we drove through the tunnel under the Swiss Alps to Turin, Italy. One humorous incident was when we parked our car under a tree in front of the hotel and the next morning upon checking out, we found we had been "greeted" by apparently several thousand birds requiring a visit to a car wash. Welcome to Italy. After an exciting drive through the French Alps we came upon the beaches of Cannes in the French Riviera. This was truly a spectacular place where the extreme wealth was appar- ent everywhere. The next day we drove through the French countryside on our way to Genoa, Italy.

Since this was August, most of the accommodations in the beach areas were already taken by visitors from Germany. We drove in-land to find lodging for the night in the town of Carcare. We liked this place very much because of the genial inhabitants, fine food, and the fact that local people played bocci ball. These local players really knew how to play the game. I know because when I was young I used to play bocci ball with my dad during the summer months when the weather was very hot but I did not mind because we were playing under a grape arbor, which my dad grew over the bocci court below.

The next day we were headed for the town of Pisa, Italy. We spent several days there enjoying the food and the sights and also taking pictures of the Tower of Pisa. Next we went to the city of Rome and spent three days in the luxury apartments in the suburbs and came back to visit the Coliseum. Needing some guidance, we inquired at a local police station for directions. One of the officers coming off her shift offered to have us follow her. Did you ever follow an Italian through the streets of Rome?

Later on we went to Naples and stayed in several pensions and hotels. At one hotel, several strangers approached us and were insistent to help with our luggage. To avoid a mounting tense situation, we decided that this was not a safe area so we moved to another hotel near the railroad station. The next day we went to the town of Pompeii and inspected the excavated areas. We did spend one day on the black sands of the beaches. From the street above, these beaches appeared like a paved asphalt surface! The locals typically covered themselves with this high-sulphur sand to cleanse themselves. After that we decided that it would be best to head north to Venice. We stayed outside of Venice in the town of Dolo. During the day we took the city bus to Venice walking the narrow streets and visiting the canals. The restaurant in the hotel where we ate our meals was also the place where we spent our evening. The location was directly across the street from a park where the festival was held. The locals were friendly and interested in hearing about where we lived in the U.S.

The next day we headed north and went to Stuttgart, Austria through the dolomite mountains. The mountain range was absolutely beautiful and so was the town of Stuttgart where we purchased a cuckoo clock characteristic of the area. After 21 days on the road we were ready to return to Frankfurt and home.

I do have some regrets about this entire vacation journey through Europe. The biggest regret that we'll always haunt me is that I never met any of the townspeople of Beho (Gouvy), Belgium. It seems I was always in a rush to make up time when I got to this town.

I have never physically stepped into the town like the other 84th division soldiers. Maybe, I will make time the next time that I am in the vicinity. I know that Jeff Neysen has returned to his town of birth and living there at this moment. I knew Jeff Neysen when he lived in Milano, Italy.

I also regret that I did not meet my father's relations when I was in the town of Anagni about 30 miles outside of Rome in the surrounding mountains. My dad, Umberto, had passed away several years before and I could not ask him who to visit or where the family resided. Anagni was a beautiful farming land.

Return to Europe #2: December 2011

Going back to "feeling the memory" of the past happenings of long ago strife is rewarding. Such was my feeling when I assisted a generous and industrious person Mr. Joseph (Jeffry) Neysen in his book entitled "Gouvy-Beho". He has just retired from his manage- rial position with the Michelin Tire Company in Milan, Italy. His account of the Battle of the Bulge, World War II, is very informative. Of course, I started to conjured up some of the things that

I did back in January, 1945. As a reward , myself and Dr. Robert Reid, a former 84th division veteran, were invited to celebrate the book signing of Mr. Neysen's book which took place on the anniversary date of the beginning Battle of the Bulge, December 17th 1944. The entire Gouvy region's population and societies dedicated their day of honor to the past hero's and deceased Americans. Dr. Reid and I (ex-Captain James V. Morgia) took part in this occasion as honored guests. I will show a few photos of many that will appeal to you. I should mention that Dr. Reid , a former mortar weapons squad leader, Company H, 335th Infantry Regiment, 84th

Infantry Division wrote his book entitled "Never Tell An Infantryman To Have A Nice Day" is well written and details his experiences with personal photos that he took during his involvement during World War II.

The next super thrill of this December, 2011 return to the Beho area, after 67 years, was the Lux-TV tour of the Battle Field, complete with snow coverage, and the meeting of Mr. Georges Nolle, a 71 year old Belgium farmer, who still lives in the Maison de Neuve Farm building complex. The last time I saw him, he was a young child scared and sheltering in the basement of the farmhouse during the attack. I found him and got him to safety. Georges Nolle was 4 years old when I met him after E Company's, 334th Infantry, 84th Division's, defense at Maison de Neuve. His dad told him all about what happened on that day of January 23, 1945. We hugged each other on Lux-TV (Retour de 2 GI's)-(December 22, 2011). I also got to sing "O Holy Night" on the Belgium national television news- what a thrill for me! It might not have been "American Idol", but I would   like to think that it was "Belgium Idol".

Recently (2015) Georges got together with the grandson,Chad Lewis, and son,Ronald Lewis, of Sgt.Roy Breaud who was with me during the defense of the Maison de Neuve. Sgt. Breaud later became head of Baton Rouge Market. The picture shows Georges and wife with the family. Another interesting development and surprise for me is that Georges wants me to come back to Beho and visit him again in the near future. God willing, after this book dis- tribution, I will make another retour to Beho area. Attached to this chapter is Mr. Ronald Lewis's Picture with his family who toured from the state of Louisiana.

Return to Europe #3: December 2014

Another great "Feeling the Memory" occurred on a subsequent Battle of the Bulge Anniversary, December 16, 2014. The generous, President and CEO, Mr. Timothy Davis, of The Greatest Genera- tion Foundation invited me and nineteen other Battle of the Bulge heroes for a ten day all expenses paid participation period in Belgium. The GGF group and staff were honored by the main events and services to remember our deceased buddies. What a country!! Even the King Philippe and his beautiful Queen Juliana partici- pated in leading the 70th anniversary of the Battle of the Bulge.

Besides the commemorative album of photographs taken during the program, I am on a Lux-Tv movie (Emissione special, Battaille de Ardennes-Lux TV (14-12-14) with the King Philippe of Belgium for about 5 minutes with many scenes about town of the famous "Nut-Day" celebration in Bastogne, Belgium, what a climax event! (attached are several photos plus TGGF letter)

The whole trip was a great adventure right from the start. I was to fly from LaGuardia airport in New York to Dulles in Washington, DC to join the Greatest Generation Foundations staff and nineteen of my fellow veterans, for a non-stop flight to Brussels, Belgium. Due to bad weather my flight was forced to land in Baltimore. I then contacted Mr. Davis who instructed me to go to Chicago's O'Hare airport and take the next flight to Brussels, Belgium which he arranged. After rescheduling and boarding the Baltimore flight to Chicago the jet had landing gear problems and subsequent deicing procedures due to snowy and icing conditions. All these precautions delayed the takeoff by one hour. To my surprise, the transatlantic jet to Brussels waited on the tarmac loaded with passengers in Chicago waiting for "little old me" to arrive.

I finally arrived at O'Hare airport fully dressed in my 70 year old original wool Captain's uniform. Everyone on my flight was ordered to remain in their seats to allow me to disembark the aircraft first to get to my connection as quickly as possible. Everyone on this flight gave me a hero's send off as I whisked by them in their seats. Next, I was motorized on a cart with two attendants speeding through the airport to the "patiently" waiting jet. Fully expecting to be greeted by angry passenger for holding up the flight for an hour much to my surprise I was greeted by cheer- ing as I rapidly moved to my seat in first class. I felt like saluting them and I did just that with gratitude. It was indeed an HONOR FLIGHT.

I later found out that the flight had pulled away from the gate and was ordered back to the gate to wait for me , it was my only hope of getting to Brussels in time for the ceremony at the American Embassy. When I landed in Brussels, I was an hour late to attend the beautiful reception for our group at the American Consulate. Everyone there was very gracious and I was finally united with my fellow veterans. This was the beginning of ten adventurous days of visiting local areas where local town people gave tribute to the deceased Americans annually. We were all honored to be a part of this tribute this year. We were housed in the Double- tree Hilton Hotel in Luxembourg City, Luxembourg.

Most of the veterans that attended The Greatest Generation Foundation event were from the famous 101 Airborne Division. I was one of the few that did not belong to this Division. The 101 was a key group that held the town of Bastogne from the German Forces. Bastogne was the key city where all the roads converged. An attached photo shows all the cross roads.

Another interesting thing happened to me in the Hilton Hotel. The Philips sisters from San Antonio, Texas were visiting and talking to all the honored veterans. One of the sisters, Faith, performed a song for the group which gave me the courage to sing a song which we both liked, "La Vie En Rose". Our impromptu performance, without rehearsal, was perfect. I must say that it was the highlight of my whole trip. I was really airborne just like the hundred first, who enjoyed the singing.

Dr. R. Reid and Capt. Morgia, Barvaux, Belgium 2011.

James & the 101st Airborne Division, Luxembourg 2014.

CHAPTER 18
THREE DAY PASS-BACK

I must admit to all you readers that this chapter could never have been written or imagined when I first started this book. Now I must write it because it is part of the whole equation. Einstein had it right, "that everything is related". You will agree when you start changing the "I's" for Eyes. Look around yourself and think about what you have read in this book about your "three day pass" to restoring yourself and the armed forces attention to preserve the morale and strength of its members. Everything in this Universal needs time to heal. Does healing make everything healthier or normal? It should if the equation is balanced. It seems that there is an unbalance on this earth because one of the components in the equation is not recycling properly. Specifically, the carbon dioxide by product of human activity cannot be absorbed or reused with the tree photo synthesis process. We must put carbon dioxide excess to work or produce less carbon dioxide to restore the natural balanced equation.

Nature has recycled this planet with a balanced equation for millions of years. It is obvious that in a mere 2000 years, especially the last 200 years of human activity, that the present carbon recycle is not natural.

It is now absolutely clear in my mind that everyone on this planet must think or mediate a solution to this huge problem which is life threatening. The theme of this book, assessing and assisting, (**DIY**) can solve the problem especially when it is performed on your three day pass or your civilian weekend. Thinking or mediating to restore yourself each weekend can also be combined to the activities to restore the planet. "Getting back to nature" will produce immediate solutions without huge payback costs for flamboyant life styles. Be an energized miser!

It is very difficult to imagine that an individual can make a big difference in the outcome of this battle. The reason why I say this is simply because pollution of the planet was caused solely by the human life on this planet Earth. The unbalance restarted when humans decided to multiply their power with the use of machines such as automobiles. The automobiles consume gasoline to power their engines. Enormous power was created when the gasoline combined with the oxygen taken from the atmosphere to produce carbon dioxide. Naturally, the trees on the planet Earth recycles the carbon dioxide to restoring oxygen. As long as the volume of carbon dioxide remained low trees were able to restore the atmosphere. The use of the combustion engine became so popular that everyone started to use it. Everyone longed for the day when they can own their own automobile and improve their lifestyle.

Use of power did not stop here, everyone started to use electricity powered appliances and light up their homes. The power industry was created to burn coal and create electricity. It was a no-brainer or an entrepreneur to use cheap natural resources to create unlim- ited energy for electricity. The trees could not extract all the carbon dioxide that was created. The excess carbon dioxide was undoubtedly absorbed by the oceans. How long can this process go on? No one can really predict the future of this scenario, so it is time to start thinking about what one can do to help mother Earth. •

James at Sikorsky inspecting equipment, circa 1972.

Made in the USA
Middletown, DE
21 February 2020

85100001R00075